The banking systems of the EU member states

The banking systems of the EU member states

Dietmar K R Klein
Translated by Henry Meyer

GRESHAM BOOKS

WOODHEAD PUBLISHING LIMITED
IN ASSOCIATION WITH
THE CHARTERED INSTITUTE OF BANKERS

Published by Gresham Books, an imprint of Woodhead Publishing Limited, Abington Hall, Granta Park, Great Abington, Cambridge CB21 6AH, UK; www.woodheadpublishing.com

Originally published in German as Die Bankensysteme der EG-Länder (2nd edition), 1992, Verlag Fritz Knapp GmbH, Frankfurt am Main, Germany, ISBN 978-3-7819-1181-9
First published in English, 1995, Woodhead Publishing Limited
Reprinted 2009

British Library Cataloguing in Publication Data
A catalogue record for this book is available from the British Library.

ISBN 978-1-85573-184-4

Printed in the United Kingdom by Lightning Source UK Limited

Contents

Preface

This book is the English version of the German book *Die Bankensysteme der EG-Länder*, which was first published by Fritz Knapp Verlag in Frankfurt am Main in 1991. This is a translation into English of the second edition, which was based on the information available in spring 1992. One of the key issues dealt with in this book is the dynamic process of transformation that European banking systems have been undergoing within an unusually brief period of time, and it should not come as a surprise that the pace of change has continued unabated. Account has therefore been taken in the English version of a number of major structural changes which have occurred in the individual banking systems of the European Union (EU) members since then.

Obviously, these revisions could not go as far as to incorporate all ongoing changes that result from new national legislation to translate European legislative measures into national law. Primarily, legislation at the European level takes the form of EC Directives, which are binding only for the various member states, but not, as such, for individual market participants there. The schematic diagram in the Introduction gives an overview, firstly, of all areas of legislation which have an impact on the banking industry in general and in which the EU Commission has taken initiatives and, secondly, of all European legislative measures ultimately adopted by the end of March 1994; finally, it also indicates all EU measures that had already been translated into German law by that date. In all member countries, quite a number of cases can be cited in which EC Directives have merely reinforced national laws and practices, or in which national legislation has been enacted and implemented ahead of mutually agreed timetables. At the same time, however, there are also some unresolved issues at the European level where even protracted negotiations have not yet led to the necessary consensus, as well as cases where national legislators are clearly lagging behind in the fulfilment of their European obligations. In addition, it is quite customary for banks and other participants in the financial markets to be granted occasionally lengthy transitional periods so as to give them adequate time to adjust as required.

In recent years, public debate in the EU member states has generally focused mainly on the pros and cons of Economic and Monetary Union (EMU), as set out in the Treaty of Maastricht. After official agreement had been reached in December 1991, the Treaty was signed in February 1992. Following a prolonged process of discussion and ratification, the Treaty finally came into effect on 1 November 1993. Indeed, the eventual commencement of the third stage of EMU, which will entail an irrevocable fixing of exchange rates, the adoption of a single monetary policy by the European Central Bank and, finally, the introduction of a single currency, will ultimately have a profound impact on banking systems of all participating member states.

The second stage of EMU, which began on 1 January 1994, has already brought about a certain number of distinct structural changes, even though responsibility for monetary policy remains vested explicitly in the national monetary authorities. The European Monetary Institute

(EMI), which is located in Frankfurt am Main and which is to operate only for a transitional period, has been entrusted with co-ordinating and advisory functions in discussions of issues of common interest to the EU central banks. Its supreme decision-making body, the EMI Council, is composed of the Governors of the EU central banks (formerly members of the Committee of EC Central Bank Governors at the Bank for International Settlements (BIS) in Basle) and the President of EMI.

The EMI's primary objective is to 'contribute to the realization of the conditions necessary for the transition to the third stage of economic and monetary union'. To this end, it is to co-ordinate and monitor the monetary policies pursued throughout the European Union. It is to prepare the technical ground for the establishment of the European System of Central Banks (ESCB), which will consist of the participating national central banks and the EMI's eventual successor, the European Central Bank (ECB). The EMI is to monitor the functioning of the EMS and will play a major role in determining the monetary policy instruments and procedures to be adopted. Eventually, it will have a key function in preparation of the decision by the EU Council of Ministers as to which countries fulfil the convergence criteria set for the move from the second to the third stage of EMU.

The commencement of the second stage itself saw the entry into force of new rules which have changed the interrelationships between the national central banks, the respective national banking systems and governments. These rules prohibit not only the financing of the public sector by the central banks (with the exception of open market operations for monetary policy purposes) but also borrowing by public entities on privileged terms from financial institutions. In anticipation of requirements to be met before the end of the second stage, three EU member states (Belgium, France and Spain) have already granted their respective central banks a large measure of independence in matters of monetary policy. In order to improve their chances of succeeding in attaining the prime goal of monetary policy, namely longer-term domestic price stability, several other member states, too, have recently given their central banks a somewhat stronger position vis-à-vis the government. No matter how important all these developments may have been, they should not divert attention from major issues which are largely, if not completely, unrelated to Maastricht.

As outlined briefly in the Introduction, strong market forces, as well as certain features of official policies, have led to an unprecedented increase not only in national and international competition in the banking sector, but also among various financial systems at the international level. By tradition, particularly in the early post-war years up to the 1960s and 1970s, the financial markets were highly protected and segmented. The European economies were highly dependent on bank loans. Only gradually did market forces begin to interact strongly with official measures to create today's competitive environment. The key developments in this context were the liberalisation of markets, deregulation in banking systems with strong barriers to universal banking, and a persistent trend towards an internationalisation of operations, which has led to global markets in wholesale banking. New communications technologies opened up previously unheard of possibilities, especially in the field of financial innovations.

Innovative instruments and features were often created in the United States to get around statutorily enforced geographic or functional segmentation there. After a certain time lag they then also gained hold in markets in Europe, either directly or via the international financial markets, although not to the same extent as in the US and rather more as an add-on. Even if there had not been an institutionalised movement towards economic convergence and integration in Europe, private sector market participants would still have had to ask themselves how to react to the new challenges without sacrificing their respective cultural identities. National supervisory and monetary authorities would still have had to respond to sweeping changes in the financial markets to ensure that they could continue to meet what was demanded of them. The key issue in this competitive environment is the question of how financial systems can best attain the objectives of efficient financial intermediation, of providing market participants with an optimum range of financial services, of keeping prices stable over longer periods, and of contributing to the stability of the financial systems. Since the mid-1980s, new types of innovative instruments in the form of derivatives (forwards, futures and options) as well as other kinds of off-balance sheet transactions involving no, or only very insignificant, cash operations have attracted great interest and added a whole new dimension – and fear – to traditional banking business. Today, derivatives have become the most powerful driving force behind desegmentation in national and international markets.

Continuous deregulation went hand in hand with new forms of regulation, above all as a result of international co-operative efforts on the part of regulators and supervisors. The goal was, and is still, to strengthen the capital base of major international 'players' and, at the same time, to make the 'playing field' more level internationally (see, in particular, the Basle Capital Accord of 1988, a set of recommendations which took full effect in 1993). Adequate responses to problems which had, in many respects, become truly international in character, could no longer be found at the national level alone, and this fact has gained increasing recognition.

In Europe, the idea of a single European financial market as part of the Common Market came strongly to the fore after the white paper on completing the internal market published in June 1985 found a favourable response. The decisive element in this respect was the Single European Act of February 1986. It placed sharp emphasis on the significance of a liberalisation of capital movements in their broadest definition. It introduced qualified majority voting in the EC Council of Ministers, and thus created the prerequisites for implementing the idea of 'Europe 1992'.

By the end of 1992, most of the European regulations needed to make the single European financial market reality had been implemented, at least at the EC level. The Second Banking Coordination Directive, which took effect on 1 January 1993, resulted in the recognition of a single licence to permit an institution to conduct finance business anywhere within the Community, and also brought the indispensable agreement on minimum standards for the mutual recognition of banks and other credit institutions. The Directive consequently established the principle of home-country supervision, with only two exceptions (liquidity and risk in the domestic market) where the country in which the respective branch is located continues to be the lead regulator.

The Second Banking Coordination Directive is supplemented by a number of related Directives. The Own Funds Directive specifies which resources qualify as capital: one tier is the owner's equity or its equivalent; another consists of subordinated debt and other similar 'hybrid' forms of capital. The Solvency Ratio Directive defines minimum ratios of capital to risk-weighted assets, under which specific risk weightings are assigned to each category of assets. The Large Exposures Directive places a ceiling of 25% of a given bank's core capital on its lending to any single borrower. Another key supplement to the basic directive is to be found in the consolidated supervision of banking conglomerates, as stipulated in the Consolidated Supervision Directive, which is likewise based on the principle of the applicability of home-country regulations.

Basically, all the aforementioned directives are geared to the model of universal banking, under which banks are permitted to conduct a broad range of activities, especially in the securities markets. The banks are largely free to decide for themselves whether to conduct such business in-house, or to do so through subsidiaries and other types of affiliated institutions, although significant exceptions to this general principle can be found in virtually all EU member states.

Some EU member states, such as the United Kingdom, still have many specialised securities firms, which are not banks in the true definition of the term, even after what has become known as the 'Big Bang' and other less far-reaching moves towards despecialisation. Such firms, too, will receive a uniform European 'passport' as soon as the Investment Services Directive, which was adopted by the EC Council of Ministers in July 1992, enters into force in 1996.

This directive is supplemented by the capital requirements set out in the Capital Adequacy Directive (CAD), which are designed to ensure that the business of dealers and brokers is both safe and sound. In line with the so-called 'building-block approach', however, the provisions of the CAD apply not only to legally independent securities houses but also to the securities trading operations of banks. For purposes of ensuring a level playing field, the CAD applies to the trading books of both banks and securities firms. To a certain extent, this will compel banks to take over some elements of the trading culture of securities houses whose capital requirements can change very rapidly in line with changing securities trading patterns, so that they can best be satisfied by a relatively high proportion of rather short term (subordinated) liabilities. Investment services are also affected by other important EC Directives.

Another issue now being discussed is the question of how not only the credit risk but also the various market risks of transactions involving derivatives, among other things, might be adequately reflected in the capital requirements imposed on both banks and other financial institutions.

All this confirms what has now been visible for quite some time. Given open financial markets, and underlying conditions marked by rising competitive pressures, the principle of mutual recognition has given way to a strengthening of the general tendency towards increasing the degree of harmonisation. In the longer run, this will be indispensable as the individual banking systems in Europe move gradually towards a true single European financial market.

Dietmar K R Klein*, Frankfurt am Main, July 1994*

Introduction

The community of twelve is spending a great deal of time and effort on implementing the idea of a single financial market. Most of the member states of the EU have already abolished whatever capital controls they had. The transitional arrangements of a temporary nature granted to the latecomers, the member states from southern Europe and Ireland, are now of only limited significance. The Council of Ministers and other EU bodies have meanwhile discussed – and in many cases already adopted – a great number of additional directives and recommendations aimed at the step-by-step implementation of an economic and monetary union.

What is essential is to enforce a minimum degree of harmonisation with respect to the regulations applicable to banks and other financial institutions. Only if that proves possible will the EU member states be prepared in full to meet the demand for free capital movements and equal treatment, i.e. free movement for banks and other financial intermediaries as well as for their clients, namely borrowers and savers, as well as other users of financial services.

The key elements of national supervision of banks with branch offices in other EU member states are to be shifted gradually from the host to the home country within the EU. This demands that the EU member states all recognise the so far only partly harmonised regulations. It will be left to increased competition between banks in the wake of the opening and progressive integration of the markets to bring about a further convergence of the competitive conditions prevailing in the individual member states.

The goal, at any rate, is to ensure that any surviving structural differences in the banking systems of the EU member states no longer give reason for similar banking transactions involving similar risks to be subject to significantly divergent requirements regarding the solvency and liquidity of the various credit institutions.

Banking structures do not change, however, only because the general legal framework in Europe converges. Technical progress, too, is a factor of competition that ensures constant change. Market shares have also been gained by those credit institutions that have made use of opportunities to expand upon the range of financial services they offer – the process of diversification. Euro-transactions, i.e. foreign currency transactions undertaken by banks with resident and non-resident clients in which the ECU, too, is used as a currency unit, increasingly lose their 'offshore' character once markets are open. They serve as substitute markets in competition with the various national currencies and financial systems.

In the course of an increased securitisation of credit relations and the growing independence of certain financial functions, the 1980s saw the emergence on the markets of a variety of new financial instruments, which are often off-balance sheet in character. They originated largely in the United States or on international financial markets. Step-by-step, many of them were adopted by market participants in Europe even in their domestic business operations. The European universal banks found themselves compelled to respond to these innovations and the threat of disintermediation either by taking defensive action in their respective home countries or, to the extent that they see themselves as 'European' or 'global' players, by actively using these new instruments in leading financial centres both inside and outside the EU.

No matter how clearly the envisaged single European financial market has already been outlined, the national banking systems in the individual EU member states still differ considerably in structure. Distinctive historical origins and diverse legal fundamentals continue to leave their mark. There are still national currencies, for which the respective national monetary authorities are responsible. Even today, however, national exchange rate policy can only be conducted within the framework of the rights and obligations provided for in the European Monetary System (EMS). Since the coming into force of the first stage of the monetary union on 1 July 1990, the central banks have been required, in line with what was set out in the Delors Plan, to meet stringent obligations for consultations with respect to their monetary policies, and to give due consideration in their measures to the interdependencies that exist in the case of open money and capital markets, as well as limited exchange rate fluctuations.

European supervisory and organisational regulations can be applied direct only to a very limited extent. In the banking sector, these regulations are usually guidelines issued in the form of directives, which are adopted by the EU Council of Ministers with a qualified majority. EU member states are required, within a predetermined period of time and with limited scope for amendments, to translate these directives into specific and directly binding national law. Other arrangements, which are not legally binding but nevertheless rather effective in the run-up to policy decisions, are the recommendations issued by the Basle Committee on Banking Supervision at the Bank for International Settlements (BIS) in Basle, Switzerland. Members of this committee are the representatives of the banking supervision authorities of not only the ten major industrial countries but also Switzerland and Luxembourg, and its recommendations have an impact on supervisory regulations and practices in other countries as well. Responsibility for banking supervision continues to be vested in the individual national authorities, even in the EU member states, although practical co-operation on individual issues of key importance has become significant within what is known as the Contact Group of EU Supervisory Authorities.

Given the opportunities available, the strategies used by individual banks and each category of bank differ rather markedly. Very few of the 10 000 or so banking institutions in the EU, including specialised banks, will be able to afford to provide both a complete range of financial services in their home countries and, at the same time, be represented throughout the territories of the other EU member states, either directly, in line with the principle of single-tier universal banking, or indirectly via subsidiaries or within holding company groups. In view of the fact that setting up new branch networks is expensive in terms of both time and money, the only way of achieving that objective will be through major mergers or acquisitions of majority holdings.

In many cases all that will be established is some form of relatively close co-operation between friendly banks, which might also include minority holdings and joint ventures. In such cases, the banks involved will set up branches and subsidiaries of their own in only a few European financial centres, and their business will be restricted to dealing with major clients.

A third alternative, which will prove the most popular in terms of the numbers involved, will see the credit institutions concentrate their activities on specific categories of clients and on certain regions. However, local banks which are members of linking systems – as is common mostly with savings banks and co-operative banks – will likewise be able to reap jointly the benefits of European co-operation via regional institutions and specialised banks (including insurance companies).

Irrespective of modern means of communication, a bank's geographic proximity to its clients will remain a key competitive advantage, at least in bulk business. What is known as relationship banking will also continue to play a major role in corporate business, even though investment banking is gaining increasing significance in the wake of both the move towards larger units of capital users with a high standing and the growing importance of major institutional investors on the financial markets.

The undifferentiated use of archetypical terms – such as that of a 'universal banking system', as opposed to that of a 'specialised banking system' – will become ever-less suitable to describe banking structures in Europe. A 'single-tier universal banking system', as is typical of Germany and a number of other continental European countries, does not, for instance, preclude some banks preferring to conduct certain securities business via separate subsidiaries. Moreover, even in Germany, supervision and corporate law requires, in principle, that typical mortgage bank and building and loan association business be conducted solely through subsidiaries. The same holds true of any insurance transactions effected in the context of 'one-stop' financing strategies, to the extent that such strategies are not aimed solely at the sale of outside insurance services, but rather at the bank–insurance tie-ups or financial conglomerates themselves supplying insurance services of their own.

Conversely, the traditional 'specialised banking system' in the United Kingdom, in which securities business was conducted by legally independent securities houses without any group affiliations, has recently been replaced by a 'multi-tier universal banking system'. Notwithstanding the fact that there are still a great number of smaller independent securities houses, the large depository institutions have been conducting securities business since

The banking systems of the EU member states

Systematic presentation of projects of significance to the banking sector in the European Union

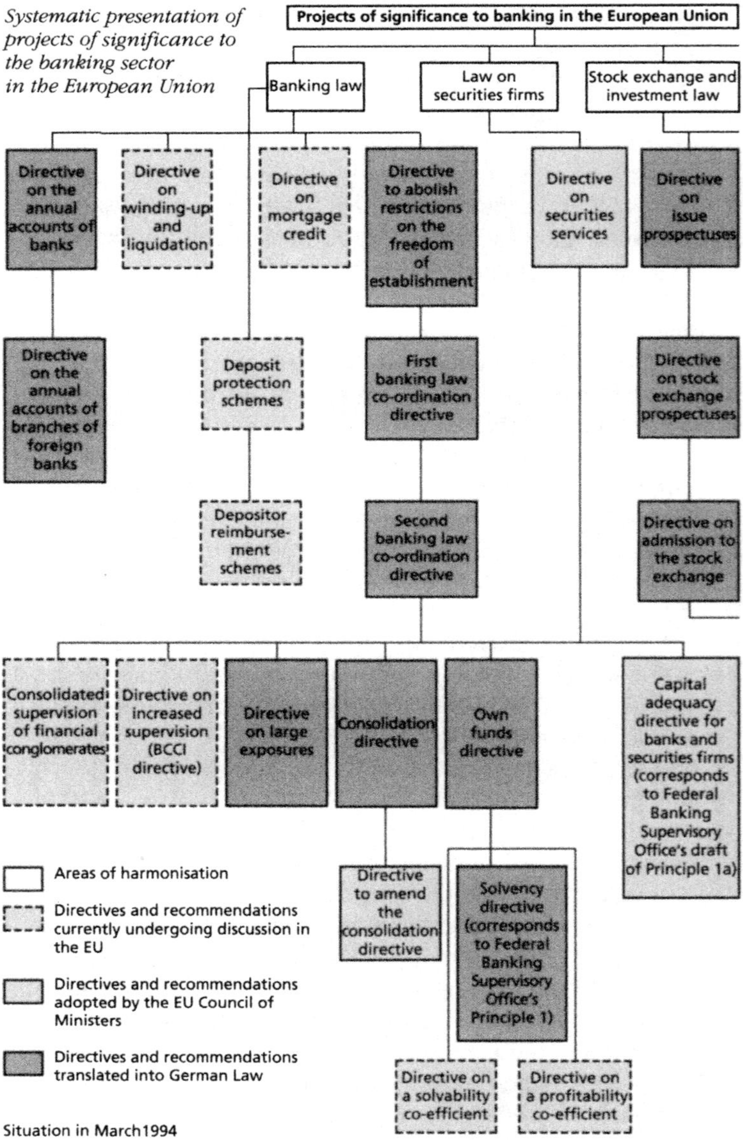

Situation in March1994

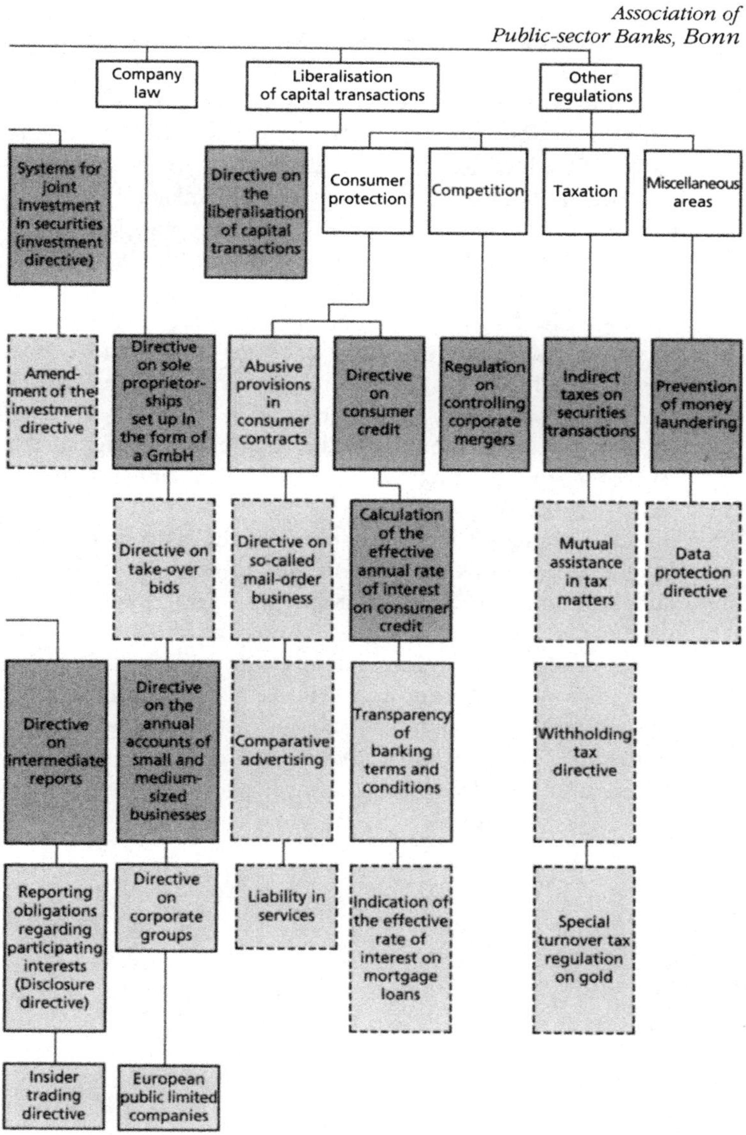
Association of
Public-sector Banks, Bonn
Company law
Liberalisation of capital transactions
Other regulations
Systems for joint investment in securities (investment directive)
Directive on the liberalisation of capital transactions
Consumer protection
Competition
Taxation
Miscellaneous areas
Amendment of the investment directive
Directive on sole proprietorships set up in the form of a GmbH
Abusive provisions in consumer contracts
Directive on consumer credit
Regulation on controlling corporate mergers
Indirect taxes on securities transactions
Prevention of money laundering
Directive on take-over bids
Directive on so-called mail-order business
Calculation of the effective annual rate of interest on consumer credit
Mutual assistance in tax matters
Data protection directive
Directive on intermediate reports
Directive on the annual accounts of small and medium-sized businesses
Comparative advertising
Transparency of banking terms and conditions
Withholding tax directive
Reporting obligations regarding participating interests (Disclosure directive)
Directive on corporate groups
Liability in services
Indication of the effective rate of interest on mortgage loans
Special turnover tax regulation on gold
Insider trading directive
European public limited companies

the 'Big Bang' of 1986, usually via subsidiaries. But the merchant banks, in particular, also effect some securities transactions directly.

This book is intended to provide a brief outline of the banking systems in the twelve EU member states in the early 1990s. It includes a short description of the structures and functions of the respective central banks and banking supervision bodies. It will be immediately apparent that this book is intended only as a first look 'behind the scenes'. It must be left to those interested to use the select bibliography to gain a greater insight into either developments in individual EU member states or specific issues, using specific monographic papers about the countries involved. This holds particularly true of the problems arising in conjunction with the gradual merging of the twelve different banking systems into a single banking market in Europe.

Also included is a description of the banks' securities business, and thus also of investment banking. Headings such as 'one-stop financing strategies' and 'financial conglomerates' require that the extension of the range of actual banking operations offered to include near-banking and even non-banking transactions be discussed as well. Capital markets and capital market institutions, as well as individual financial instruments, by contrast, were not deemed to be within the scope of this book.

1 Germany

General outline

By tradition, the credit system in Germany is marked by universal-type banks. At the end of 1989, the share of universal banks in the total business volume of all credit institutions (excluding building and loan associations) came to some 78%. As most private sector mortgage banks, which belong to the category of specialised banks, not only have capital links to the big banks and regional banks but are often also part of a corporate group, the significance of universal banks in Germany today is even greater than that indicated by the figures showing their market share. Intense competition has led to a strengthening of the trend towards diversification in the 1980s. The supply of services on offer has been broadened to include both new, off-balance sheet banking operations and new products which, although they are not banking transactions as defined in section 1 of the Gesetz über das Kreditwesen *((KWG) Banking Act), are more or less near-banking operations.*

For instance, included among these new products are real estate placement activities in conjunction with mortgage business, the management of private financial assets, corporate consultancy services and cash management operations for industrial enterprises. In the wake of the wave of securitisation in the 1980s, banks' own-account trading in securities, which – unlike securities business for the accounts of third parties – is not deemed banking business as defined in section 1 of the KWG, has gained considerable significance. Building and loan associations as well as life insurance companies have secured a steadily growing proportion of households' total savings, while universal banks have not been permitted to conduct either building and loan association or life insurance business themselves, though they have gained increased access to such business indirectly. Common distribution channels have been the norm for some time now; recent years have seen an increase both in the reciprocal capital links between banks and insurance companies, and in the establishment by banks of new subsidiaries active in insurance as well as building and loan association business.

The share of credit institutions in the total gross value added by all economic sectors in Germany has risen since the 1960s, and now exceeds 4%. At the end of 1989, the banking sector employed 631 000 persons, i.e. 2.2% of the total labour force. This number rose further to 694 000 by the end of 1990, with 49 000 being employed in the new Länder *(the* Länder *or Federal States created in the territory of the former GDR after its merger with West Germany). Mergers have caused the number of credit institutions, mostly in the co-operative banking sector but also – though to a far lesser extent – in the savings and commercial banking sectors, to contract significantly over the past few decades. At the end of 1989, there were some 4300 credit institutions engaged in banking business as defined in section 1 of the KWG, virtually all of which regularly submit reports for the Monthly Balance Sheet Statistics, as against some 13 000 institutions thirty years ago (excluding postal giro and postal savings bank offices in both cases). The mergers were aimed at creating larger operating units in the wake of both the professionalisation of the co-operative banking system and the adjustment of the savings banking sector to the redrawing of local authorities' areas of jurisdiction. The number of bank outlets, by contrast, continued to rise significantly up until the beginning of the 1980s, although it has declined again slightly since then. At the end of 1989, the number of bank branch offices in Germany totalled 44 156, so that there was about one for every 1400 people. Including the credit institutions in the new* Länder *– the establishment of which had brought a one-off increase of about one-tenth in 1990 – the total number of institutions climbed to 4453 by the end of 1991, and the number of domestic branch offices, including main offices, rose to 49 325. The number of cash dispensers linked to the banking sector's overall interbank network came to some 5160 at the end of 1988.*

The number of cheque cards issued under the Eurocheque system totalled 21.7 million, thereby accounting for half of all the European bank clients using that system. Among the credit cards available in Germany, Eurocard, which is issued by the German banks and which can be used worldwide as a result of co-operation agreements concluded with the US credit card system MasterCard and the British credit card group Access, plays a leading role, with 960 000 cards in circulation.

Structure and functions of the Deutsche Bundesbank

At the top of the German banking system stands the Deutsche Bundesbank as the bankers' bank, the bank of issue and the central bank, which is also responsible, together with the Bundesaufsichtsamt für das Kreditwesen (Federal Banking Supervisory Office) in Berlin, for key banking supervision functions. The Deutsche Bundesbank is owned by the federal government. Until October 1992, it consisted of the Direktorium (central office) in Frankfurt am Main, eleven Hauptverwaltungen (main offices, also known as 'Landeszentralbanken', i.e. Land Central Banks), with one situated in each of the old *Länder*, and – since mid-1990 – a Vorläufige Verwaltungsstelle (provisional administrative office) in eastern Berlin. Since 1 November 1992, the Bundesbank has had 175 branches and sub-branches in western Germany as well as 15 branches in eastern Germany. As stipulated in the *Gesetz über die Deutsche Bundesbank* (BBkG or Deutsche Bundesbank Act) of 1957, its supreme decision-making body is the Zentralbankrat (Central Bank Council). This body determines the Bundesbank's monetary and credit policies, and decides on general guidelines for its management and administration. The Central Bank Council comprises the Members of the Board of the Deutsche Bundesbank and the Presidents of the Land Central Banks.

The reorganisation of the Bundesbank to incorporate the five new *Länder*, as is required under the provisions of the *Einigungsvertrag* (the unification treaty governing the merger between East and West Germany), ultimately entered into force on 1 November 1992. The *Änderungsgesetz* (Amendment Act) provides for the number of Land Central Banks, and so that of their representatives in the Central Bank Council, to be reduced from 11 to 9, even though the number of *Länder* in Germany has now risen to 16. At the same time, the maximum number of Members of the Board of the Deutsche Bundesbank was cut from 10 to 8 (in addition to the President and Vice-President, there are currently only 5 additional Members of the Board).

The President at the head of the Board of the Deutsche Bundesbank is merely first among equals. The Members of the Board of the Deutsche Bundesbank are appointed, usually for a period of eight years, by the President of the Federal Republic of Germany, upon the proposal of the federal government and after consulting the Central Bank Council. The Presidents of the Land Central Banks are appointed upon the proposal of the Bundesrat – the second chamber of the German Parliament representing the *Länder* – on the basis of suggestions submitted by the respective *Länder* governments. The key to the far-reaching legal and factual autonomy of the Bundesbank is to be found, above all, in the provisions of section 12 of the BBkG, under which the central bank is required, without prejudice to the performance of its functions, to support the federal government's general economic policy, but is independent of instructions from the federal government in exercising the powers conferred on it by that Act.

Under the provisions of section 3 of the BBkG, the Bundesbank is responsible for regulating both the amount of money in circulation and the volume of credit supplied to the economy in such a way that the currency is safeguarded, and for arranging for the handling by banks of domestic and external payments. Safeguarding the currency must be understood primarily as the maintenance of domestic price stability over time. The Bundesbank has the sole right to issue banknotes. In exercising its monetary policy powers, it fixes the discount rate at which it is prepared, for purposes of managing both the liquidity of banks and the money market rates, to purchase trade bills eligible for rediscount at the Bundesbank from the credit institutions. The ceiling on such bill purchases is defined individually for each credit institution in what are known as rediscount quotas. In principle, there is no ceiling on Lombard loans, which are granted to credit institutions at the usually higher (between 1% and 2%) Lombard rate against the collateral of special federal treasury bills and appropriately eligible bonds. Lombard loans are intended only to help overcome very short term liquidity bottlenecks.

In order to bring influence to bear on the money market, the Bundesbank is entitled to buy and sell certain bills, federal treasury bills, federal treasury certificates and marketable bonds. Within the scope of such open market operations, what are known as securities transactions under repurchase agreements have gained considerable significance in the last few years. In such transactions, the Bundesbank uses tenders at fixed terms but variable interest rates (interest rate tenders) or at a fixed interest rate (volume tenders) to purchase certain securities for short periods of nowadays usually two or four weeks, subject to the seller buying the securities back forward at the same time. The rates for securities repurchase transactions have meanwhile assumed a basing function on the money market. Supported, where necessary, by further fine-tuning measures, such as very short term securities repurchase agreements or the shifting of short term federal and *Länder* government deposits to the commercial banks, this allows the Bundesbank to influence actively the money market rates.

The Bundesbank's interest rate and liquidity policy is aimed at keeping the growth of the broadly defined money stock M3 (currency in circulation, sight deposits, time deposits and funds borrowed for less than four years plus savings deposits at statutory notice) within specific limits over the medium term. This intermediate monetary target along the road towards the ultimate goal of achieving price stability, which is valid for the subsequent twelve months, is defined by the Central Bank Council in December each year.

Another instrument used to influence the liquidity of the credit institutions and their potential credit creation is the requirement to maintain minimum reserves in the order of a certain percentage of the deposits of both domestic non-banks and non-residents. They must be held in the form of average monthly non-interest bearing balances at the Bundesbank. The expansion of the liquid bank deposits as part of M3 automatically leads to an increased need for liquidity, so that the credit institutions are compelled, *ceteris paribus*, to use the Bundesbank as the lender of last resort.

The minimum reserve ratios may differ, depending on the type of deposit involved. The ratios were changed relatively rarely in the last few years. The limited effectiveness of minimum reserve policy in the case of open markets, international competition and a Euro-market which is largely free of minimum reserve requirements has resulted, *inter alia*, in relatively low ratios for time deposits of both residents and non-residents. After they had remained unchanged at 4.95% since 1 February 1987, they were cut further to 2%, across the board, on 1 March 1993. One year later, the ratio for sight deposits was likewise reduced substantially, from 12.1% to 5%, so that the required reserves were brought down to a level not much higher than that which the banks must maintain anyway in the form of working balances. Non-residents' foreign currency liabilities are exempt from the minimum reserve requirements to the extent that the funds borrowed in international interbank business, for instance, are reinvested abroad.

Of great significance to its monetary policy is also the power of the Bundesbank to buy and sell payment media denominated in foreign currencies. Such transactions have an impact not only on the exchange rates but also on the liquidity of the banks. Whereas the Bundesbank is basically free (*vis-à-vis* the US dollar, the leading intervention currency) to decide whether or not to leave developments to the exchange markets themselves or whether to intervene on a case-by-case basis, it is obliged to comply with existing intervention rules with respect to the currencies of the EMS member countries.

These rules, which were adopted in 1979, required the Bundesbank, as a member of the EMS intervention system, to ensure that actual exchange rates did not deviate more than 2¼% up or down from the bilateral central rates. (Spain, which became a member of the Exchange Rate Mechanism (ERM) in June 1989, and the United Kingdom, which joined it in October 1990, still had a broader margin of ±6%, while Greece and Portugal – which became a member in April 1992 – whose currencies were likewise included in the European basket currency ECU on a pro rata basis, did not participate in the intervention system.) Most of the interventions, however, took place even before the predetermined intervention marks were reached. After the EMS crisis, the United Kingdom and Italy withdrew from the ERM on 17 September 1992. In the wake of the second crisis on 2 August 1993, the remaining participants in the ERM raised the permissible intervention margin to ±15%, with the exception of the bilateral margin between the Deutsche Mark and the Dutch guilder, which remained at $\pm 2\frac{1}{4}$%.

The fact that the Deutsche Mark has been the most important and most stable EMS currency in recent years has enabled it to strengthen the position it factually holds as the system's anchor. In addition to the US dollar, the other EMS currencies and the ECU, the EMS partner countries are making increased use of the Deutsche Mark as a reserve and intervention currency. In contrast to the private ECU, which has gained considerable ground on the international financial markets, the official ECU is largely of only symbolic significance. At the centre of common exchange rate realignments stand changes in the bilateral central rates; in a second step, the new ECU rates are then merely derived from the changes in the bilateral rates. The endeavours undertaken by the EMS partner countries to bring their monetary policies into line with that pursued by the Bundesbank, and thus to improve the convergence between their economies and that of Germany, are the reason why – until mid-September 1992 – there had not been any general realignment of exchange rates since the beginning of 1987. Another factor in this, however, was the exceptionally heavy burden associated with the economic integration of the former GDR into a larger, unified Germany, which basically weakened the German currency.

The main reason why it was ultimately impossible to keep the central rate pattern unchanged was an increasing lack of convergence, as demonstrated by not only the cumulative price differentials *vis-à-vis* the Deutsche Mark, but also by the high level of short term interest rates in Germany, which were essential to combat inflationary expectations. Second thoughts about the prospects of economic and monetary union in Europe, as envisaged in the Maastricht Treaty, had a certain impact as well.

Finally, the Bundesbank is required to fulfil additional functions, which are either mentioned expressly in the Deutsche Bundesbank Act – as in the case of its activities as the fiscal agent of the federal government, for instance – or derived rather indirectly from its functions as a monetary policy decision-making institution, because it needs a properly functioning banking system as well as orderly money and capital market situations to carry out its tasks.

Legislation and banking supervision

As stipulated in detail in the KWG, the Bundesbank also has major tasks to fulfil within the scope of banking supervision, although prime responsibility in this respect is vested in the Federal Banking Supervisory Office in Berlin. The *Grundsätze über das Eigenkapital und die Liquidität der Kreditinstitute* (Principles Concerning the Capital and Liquidity of Credit Institutions), which fleshes out the framework set by the provisions of the Banking Act, can only be adopted and amended in agreement with the Bundesbank.

At the Land Central Bank level, the Bundesbank has also been given major functions with regard to the practical implementation of banking supervision, such as the review of the various reports which credit institutions are required to submit. These include annual accounts as well as reports on large loans, previously of one million Deutsche Marks or more but now three million Deutsche Marks or more, as well as loans to managers, etc, individual and consolidated monthly returns, reports on country risks, etc. The Bundesbank is also responsible for the evaluation of the audits carried out by external accounting firms. Under the provisions of section 7 of the KWG, the Bundesbank and the Federal Banking Supervisory Office are required, in a spirit of co-operation, to inform each other of any observations or findings that might be of significance to the fulfilment of their mutual tasks. Along with members of the federal government in issues of monetary policy, the President of the Federal Banking Supervisory Office, too, is entitled to participate, albeit without a right to vote, in the meetings of the Central Bank Council whenever matters falling in his sphere of responsibility are discussed.

The Banking Act of 1961 is the most important act governing the structure of the banking sector and banking supervision. Since then, it has been amended repeatedly, most recently and rather extensively in 1984–85, when the principle of consolidation was introduced with respect to the requirements regarding both liable capital and large exposures. The amalgamation of a banking institution with its domestic and foreign subsidiaries (as from a participating interest of 40%) into a banking group is to prevent the parent institution's capital from being used as a cushion several times over, and thus to ensure that the group's lending business and other solvency risks are adequately secured. Accordingly, the credit institutions' reporting obligations with regard to monthly returns, reports on large loans, the drawing up and publication of annual accounts and annual reports, and quarterly reports on country risks were extended to include banking groups.

A licence issued by the Federal Banking Supervisory Office is required to conduct banking business. The Banking Act is based on a broad definition of universal banking, insofar as there are no specialised banks which have been assigned the exclusive right in special legislation to conduct certain banking transactions. An enterprise is deemed to be a credit institution if it performs, as a commercial undertaking, only one of the nine banking operations set out in section 1 of the KWG, namely deposit business, lending business, discount business, securities business, safe custody business, investment fund business, the incurrence of the obligation to acquire claims in respect of loans prior to their maturity, guarantee business and giro business.

As also holds true of some other near-banking transactions, factoring, forfeiting and leasing, money changing activities as well as buying and selling securities for one's own account are therefore not banking operations which require licensing by the Federal Banking Supervisory Office, even though they are often performed by banks either directly or via subsidiaries. What is vital is that appropriate authorisation is essential to conduct any one of the operations listed in section 1 of the KWG, while the British system deems the definition of a credit institution to be met only if lending and borrowing business is conducted. Any credit institution of the universal type is therefore entitled to execute securities transactions for its clients. It is free to decide itself, however, which generally approved banking transactions it wishes to perform and which functions it wishes to assume direct or via subsidiaries.

A licence may be refused only for one of the reasons listed in the Banking Act. The most important of these grounds for refusal are inadequate capital resources, managers lacking the necessary personal and professional qualifications and a violation of the principle of dual control. A lack of demand for the business in question, however, is not a reason for withholding a banking licence. The Federal Banking Supervisory Office has far-reaching powers to intervene and counter irregularities in banking. Included are the rights to remove managers from office, to revoke a licence and to petition for compulsory liquidation. However, in the event of crises which affect the entire banking sector and which warrant expectations of grave dangers to the economy as a whole, only the federal government is entitled, through the issue of a statutory order, to impose a moratorium on or to halt banking and stock exchange operations.

The obligations of credit institutions to submit reports and provide information are set out in detail in the regulations. Certified accountants are required to review at least once a year whether not only the provisions of both the Banking Act and a number of special acts for specific categories of banks, such as the *Hypothekenbankgesetz* (Mortgage Bank Act) and the *Bausparkassengesetz* (Act on Building and Loan Associations), but also the accounting rules, for instance, have been complied with. Depending on the legal form of establishment of the institution concerned, accounting rules are laid down in various laws: the *Handelsgesetzbuch* or HGB (Commercial Code), the *Aktiengesetz* (Companies Act), the *GmbH-Gesetz* (Act on Private Limited Companies – in this case, in the form of the *Bilanzrichtliniengesetz* (Act Concerning the Fourth, Seventh and Eighth EC Council Directives on the Annual Accounts of Certain Types of Companies) of 1985), the *Publizitätsgesetz* (Act on Data Disclosure), in corresponding *Länder* legislation on savings banks and in special regulations on the forms to be used.

On 10 February 1992, a *Verordnung über die Rechnungslegung der Kreditinstitute* (RechKredV, or Regulation on the Accounts of Credit Institutions) was issued on the basis of the *Bankbilanzrichtlinie-Gesetz* (Act Concerning the EC Council Bank Annual Accounts Directive) of 30 November 1990. It had to be applied for the first time to annual accounts and annual reports as well as to consolidated annual accounts and group annual reports for the financial year commencing 31 December

1992. It replaced the former *Verordnung über Formblätter für die Gliederung des Jahresabschlusses von Kreditinstituten* (Regulation on the Forms to be used for the Breakdown of the Annual Accounts of Credit Institutions), as amended on 14 September 1987, and marked the translation into national law of both the EC Directive of December 1986 on the annual and consolidated accounts of banks and other financial establishments and the EC Directive of February 1989 on the publication of the accounts of branches in a member state by credit institutions and financial establishments with their head offices outside that member state.

The core of the Banking Act is formed by the provisions on the capital and liquidity of credit institutions, as stipulated in section 10ff of the KWG. The requirements are set out in detail in the *Grundsätze über das Eigenkapital und die Liquidität der Kreditinstitute* (Principles Concerning the Capital and Liquidity of Credit Institutions), which were developed by the Federal Banking Supervisory Office in agreement with the Bundesbank. Specifically, the banks and banking groups have to be adequately endowed with liable capital, which must be in proportion to the risk-weighted assets on the balance sheet (Principle I prescribes a ratio of 1:18). The foreign exchange risks are limited by Principle Ia, while the banks' liquidity is to be secured by means of a predetermined ratio of long or short-term assets to the factually corresponding resources on the liabilities side of the balance sheet.

With effect from October 1990, the provisions of Principles I and Ia were extended in anticipation of the partly already adopted and, at that time, partly still controversial EU capital requirements for banks and securities firms. Included are now also the counterparty risk as well as the foreign exchange, interest rate and other price risks of the banks' so-called off-balance sheet transactions, the significance of which has been rising rapidly since the late 1980s, even in Germany. Additional capital requirements are triggered direct only by the extension of Principle I, while the parallel provisions of Principle Ia merely impose a ceiling on the level of the open items in terms of the capital, irrespective of the requirements set out in Principle I.

Market shares of the individual categories of banks

According to the statistics of the Bundesbank, 96% of the total number of 4297 credit institutions (including building and loan associations as well as other categories of banks not covered by the monthly balance sheet statistics) in Germany at the end of 1989 were universal banks. Even though almost 500 additional banks from the former GDR had joined the West German banking system, the total figure declined to 4200 credit institutions by the end of 1992. Viewed on the basis of the monthly balance sheet statistics, they accounted for 78% of the total business volume. The universal banks, which are often also referred to as commercial banks, can be broken down into three major categories:

private law commercial banks with a share of about 32% in the total business volume of all commercial banks;

public law banks, such as savings banks and regional giro institutions, with a share of almost 48%;

co-operative credit institutions, i.e. the People's Banks and Raiffeisen Banks as well as their regional institutions, with a share of just over 20%.

Although the credit institutions in these three categories are all basically universal banks of the continental European type, the core business of the individual categories continues to differ rather markedly.

The category of specialised banks encompasses private and public law mortgage banks, banks with special functions, the postal giro and postal savings bank offices as well as the building and loan associations, which are dealt with separately. Not included in the monthly balance sheet statistics are investment companies, central securities depositories and guarantee banks (see Table 1).

Private law commercial banks

This category of bank, which includes 321 private law commercial banks, is very heterogeneous in structure. At the top stand the three big banks, Deutsche Bank AG, Dresdner Bank AG and Commerzbank AG, each of which had an independent subsidiary in West Berlin (at least until the end of 1990). The big three banks are large chains with country-wide networks encompassing 3110 branch offices between them. Their origins date back to the establishment of the German Reich in 1871.

The common stock of the big banks is widely dispersed. The numbers of resident and non-resident shareholders range from 160 000 to 310 000, and these figures include considerable numbers of staff. The big three banks all belong to the top group of equity-strong banks not just in Europe (see Appendix 1) but also worldwide, even though they differ significantly in terms of both size and earnings power. At the end of 1989, the consolidated balance sheet total of the Deutsche Bank AG came to DM 344 billion, as against the DM 250 billion of the Dresdner Bank AG and the DM 192 billion of the Commerzbank AG. If the unconsolidated annual accounts (including the respective subsidiaries in Berlin, however) are used as a basis, the balance sheet totals of these three banks were DM 225 billion, DM 155 billion and DM 134 billion, respectively.

The three big banks all have a comprehensive range of financial, investment and other services on offer, either direct or via subsidiaries. Their true significance is not fully

Table 1 *The German banking system (at the end of 1989)*

	Business volume		Loans to non-banks		Deposits of non-banks			
	DM billion	%	DM billion	%	DM billion	%	Credit institutions	Domestic branch offices
Commercial banks	1063.9	24.9	670.6	25.7	459.0	21.9	321	6 286
Big banks	410.0	9.6	266.6	10.2	223.3	10.6	6	3 110
Regional and other commercial banks	505.9	11.8	341.5	13.1	200.1	9.5	169	2 821
Branches of foreign banks	81.5	1.9	23.8	1.0	5.7	0.3	60	34
Private banks	66.5	1.6	38.7	1.5	30.0	1.4	86	321
Regional giro institutions	662.8	15.5	355.4	13.6	144.7	6.9	11	219
Savings banks	915.8	21.4	591.1	22.7	684.7	32.6	583	17 359
Regional institutions of credit co-operatives	184.1	4.3	54.5	2.1	12.6	0.6	4	32
Credit co-operatives	523.2	12.2	323.6	12.4	416.3	19.8	3223	15 789
Mortgage banks	576.5	13.5	435.5	16.7	214.4	10.2	37	38
Private law mortgage banks	437.3	10.2	326.5	12.5	133.2	6.3	28	32
Public law mortgage banks	139.3	3.3	109.0	4.2	31.2	3.9	9	6
Banks with special functions	289.8	6.8	147.4	5.7	109.0	5.2	16	84
Postal giro and postal savings bank offices	61.4	1.4	29.8	1.1	58.3	2.8	...	...

Building and loan associations[1]	161.0		133.3		124.5		21	50
Private law building and loan associations	110.3		91.7		87.6		18	50
Public law building and loan associations	50.8		41.6		36.9		3[2]	...
Categories of banks not included in the monthly balance sheet statistics								
Investment companies	...	...	...	...	...	...	51	3
Central securities depositories	...	...	...	...	...	...	2	1
Guarantee banks and other credit institutions	...	...	...	...	...	...	28	...
Total	**4272.5**	**100**	**2 608.0**	**100**	**2 098.9**	**100**	**4 297**	**39 861**
Memorandum item								
Credit institutions in which majority interests are held by								
non-resident banks	115.8		56.0		27.9		68	433
non-resident non-banks	...	...	...	...	...	...	34	55

Source: Monthly Reports of the Deutsche Bundesbank *(Tables III 13, 14 and 26).*

1 Business volume not included in the total.

2 Excluding the nine legally dependent Länder *building and loan associations.*

reflected in their aggregate business volume, which accounts for only just under 10% of the total business volume of all domestic credit institutions. Including their mortgage bank and other domestic banking subsidiaries, their share in the total volume of banking business amounted to 17%. In the field of off-balance sheet business, which has expanded rapidly since the mid-1980s, they account for a far larger proportion, with roughly 50% of all off-balance sheet interest and currency swaps. They process almost 60% of all Germany's external payments, arrange for around half of the loans raised and bond issues placed on the domestic market and manage more than 40% of all securities deposits. The big banks play a major role in construction finance, either direct or via subsidiaries, and have participating interests in specialised banks such as mortgage banks and, more recently, building and loan associations.

In order to counter competition from the life insurance companies, the big banks extended their range of services towards the end of the 1980s to include old-age pension schemes within the scope of one-stop financing strategies, as had been done before not only by the savings and co-operative banks in appropriate linking systems but also by a number of regional banks. The life insurance products of the insurance sector are usually involved in their range of services. The Deutsche Bank has established a life insurance subsidiary of its own and has also acquired a majority stake in another insurance group, both of which are subject to separate supervision by the Bundesaufsichtsamt für das Versicherungswesen (Federal Supervisory Office for Insurance Enterprises) in Berlin.

Finally, what is also of special significance is the systematic extension of the strong presence of the three big banks throughout Europe and the world (see separate section below).

The category of regional and other commercial banks encompasses all other commercial banks which have been established in the legal form of either an *Aktiengesellschaft* (AG – public limited company), a *Kommanditgesellschaft auf Aktien* (KGaA – limited company with one or more general partners) or a *Gesellschaft mit beschränkter Haftung* (GmbH – private limited company), but which are not represented to the same nationwide extent in Germany and which have in part restricted their business operations to certain types of transactions. Closest in status to the big three are the Bayerische Hypotheken- und Wechselbank AG and the Bayerische Vereinsbank AG, both of which have their headquarters in Munich. A peculiarity they share with the Norddeutsche Hypotheken- und Wechselbank AG is that they belong to the category of mixed mortgage banks which have the right, in addition to that of conducting general banking business, to grant mortgage and communal loans and to issue *Pfandbriefe* (mortgage bonds) and communal bonds for that purpose. Third in the list of the regional banks is the BfG Bank AG, formerly the Bank für Gemeinwirtschaft AG. It was wholly but indirectly owned by the trade unions until the end of 1986, when the Aachener und Münchner Versicherungsgruppe (an insurance group) acquired a participating interest of 50% plus one share. The BfG Bank AG has meanwhile been taken over by Crédit Lyonnais, the largest commercial bank in France. The fourth-largest regional bank is the Berliner Bank AG, which has most of its branch offices in Berlin but is also represented in major financial centres in western and eastern Germany and has participating interests in subsidiaries dealing in small client and mortgage business. In 1993, it became the core bank of Bankgesellschaft Berlin, which is also the owner of, among other things, the public sector Landesbank Berlin.

The BHF-Bank KGaA, Berlin/Frankfurt, which was established as a result of a merger between the Berliner Handels-Gesellschaft and the Frankfurter Bank, is very similar to an internationally operating merchant bank.

Worth mentioning are some of the larger regional banks, such as the Westfalenbank AG, Bochum/Düsseldorf, and the Vereins- und Westbank AG in Hamburg (which is now part of the Bayerische Vereinsbank group). Business with non-residents is the speciality of a number of *Überseebanken* (overseas banks), such as the Deutsch-Südamerikanische Bank AG in Hamburg, a wholly-owned subsidiary of the Dresdner Bank AG, and the Ibero-Amerika Bank AG in Bremen, while the former European Asian Bank (the successor of the Deutsch-Asiatische Bank AG) has meanwhile been integrated completely into the Deutsche Bank AG.

At the end of 1989, a category of banks with a long tradition in Germany – private banks – amounted to only 86 institutions with a total of 321 outlets. Such banks are operated in the legal form of either a sole proprietorship (a form of establishment which has not been permitted since the introduction of the principle of dual control in 1976), a general or limited partnership or a family-owned limited company with one or more general partners. Viewed in terms of the consolidated business volume, the leading private bank is the Bankhaus Sal Oppenheim jr & Cie in Cologne/Frankfurt. The private banks deal mainly in securities, and arrange usually for short term foreign trade financing, industrial finance, asset management and real estate business.

Presence of foreign financial institutions in Germany

Recent years have seen an increased move to Germany by banks from all over the world, even though the federal government has always refused to promote its home market in the sense of an offshore financial centre. The stability and soundness of the liberal German economic and monetary system as well as the relative size of the domestic market within the European Union – a factor that has gained considerable significance in the wake of German reunification in 1990 – and the openness of the financial markets after the abolition of remaining impediments are making Germany increasingly attractive to financial institutions from abroad. Their presence has improved Germany's competitive position as a financial centre, the core of which lies in Frankfurt am Main, and has stimulated increased competition in the banking sector.

At the end of 1989, more than 300 foreign institutions had established offices of some kind or other in Germany. 60 of these institutions were foreign banks which had together opened a total of 94 branches on the domestic market. A further 68 credit institutions incorporated in Germany, in which foreign banks have majority holdings and which are regarded in statistics as a distinct category of banks, were represented with an additional 433 branch offices, i.e. they had 501 bank outlets in total. A category not identified separately in banking statistics is gaining increasing significance, namely that of domestic credit institutions in which non-resident non-banks have majority interests; the 34 institutions involved include not only subsidiaries of foreign production and distribution companies but also major investment banks, primarily from the United States and Japan, which – given the functional separation in the financial services sectors there – are not deemed to be banks in the true definition of the term in their home countries. In addition, 172 institutions maintained a total of 327 representative offices.

Together, the three categories conducting banking business had a share of some 5% in the total business volume of all credit institutions in Germany. Viewed solely in terms of the category of commercial banks, their market share was four times higher. As foreign banks also have a great number of minority holdings in Germany, and as the representative offices initiate numerous cross-border transactions, the overall involvement of non-residents in the

German financial market is even greater than that recorded statistically. Fee-generating business, such as investment banking and external transactions, stand in the foreground of that involvement. In view of their narrow client deposit base, the foreign banks rely on the national and international interbank markets for the refinancing of their predominantly wholesale lending business. Just under 30% of the total business volume of all banks controlled from abroad was accounted for by institutions from the United States, while Japanese and French institutions had shares of some 20% and about 10%, respectively.

Branches and subsidiaries of German credit institutions abroad

The activities of German banks abroad have developed particularly dynamically; given the loss of all their foreign branches and subsidiaries after the Second World War, the German credit institutions had to make a completely fresh start. While initial interest in the establishment of offices abroad had, since the end of the 1960s, focused on Luxembourg, where German banks could use their subsidiaries to conduct primarily Euro-Deutsche Mark business both with clients in third countries and with companies in Germany without that business being subject to minimum reserve requirements, it was London, with investment banking as the core business, that came increasingly to the fore in the 1980s.

Transactions executed via subsidiaries abroad have increased in relative importance. However, the example set by the establishment of Deutsche Bank Capital Markets Limited in London shows that the banks' decisions on the legal form of establishment were by no means uniform. In 1992, however, when Deutsche Bank AG acquired Morgan Grenfell Ltd, a major investment bank, that subsidiary was closed down and its business transferred largely to the branch office in London. In the early stages of the internationalisation of banking business, the banks often made do with minority stakes in joint undertakings, which were referred to as 'banking syndicates'. This form of conducting banking business has lost much of its appeal, however, because it gave rise to conflicts of interest and problems of identification in relations with parent banks.

The leading credit institutions' need to establish a presence throughout the world made other leading financial centres, such as New York, Tokyo, Singapore and Hong Kong, gain increasing significance as well. German banks have always followed in the footsteps of their German clients. For some time now, the leading German banks have been endeavouring increasingly also to establish a presence in other financial centres in Europe. At the time of writing, the Deutsche Bank (taking over Banca d'America e d'Italia SpA (BAI) of Italy and acquiring a majority interest in Comercial Transatlántico in Spain) and, on a far more modest scale, the Dresdner Bank (acquiring Banque Veuve Morin-Pons SA in Paris) have been successful examples of the acquisition of majority interests in banks located in other European countries to gain access to their branch networks, and to be able to enter retail banking business there.

At the end of 1989, the combined business volume of the 87 foreign subsidiaries totalled DM 262 billion, a figure which had risen to DM 371 billion by the end of 1992, with almost two thirds being accounted for by the Luxembourg subsidiaries alone. The expansion of business was particularly sharp in 1988 and 1989, when German enterprises and individuals shifted a larger proportion of their time deposits to accounts abroad. In addition, 26 German credit institutions with 118 foreign branch offices had a business volume abroad that came to DM 297 billion (excluding their business with their headquarters and branch offices in Germany) and that increased further to DM 470 billion by the end of 1992. At the end of 1989, the total business volume processed via foreign branches and subsidiaries was equal to some 13% of that executed by all German banks, and to just over 100% of Germany's total business with non-residents.

Savings banks and regional giro institutions

The savings banks and their regional giro institutions which – with only a few exceptions – belong to the category of public law credit institutions, have gained significance over the decades. The prevalent principle that the domestic activities of savings banks be restricted to specific regions, and their need to avoid losing out on any market and earnings potentials at home, makes these banks concentrate their universal banking activities on the domestic market. Recently, however, both the creation of the single European market and the stiffening of competition in an environment ruled by free market economy principles have increasingly given rise to critical questions as to the future role of the savings banks and the separation of functions in the system linking the savings banks and the '*Landesbanken*' (regional giro institutions).

At the end of 1989, such public law universal banks accounted for some 37% of the total business volume of all credit institutions. Most of the 583 savings banks are public law entities endowed with legal capacity of their own. Their guarantors are primarily local, municipal and district authorities. By tradition, their core business is to be found in deposit-taking on the liabilities side, and in conventional lending on the assets side, while both external and securities transactions are generally of minor significance. Only 11 of the institutions are what are known as *Freie Sparkassen* (independent savings banks); this category, however, includes some of the largest institutions and accounts for roughly 8% of the savings banks' consolidated balance sheet total.

Today, the savings banks, in co-operation with the regional giro institutions, execute all banking transactions that are typical of universal banks. It was as early as 1908 that the *Scheckgesetz* (Cheque Act) gave them the right to act as drawees of cheques, thus enabling them to conduct sight and demand deposit business. The savings banks are still subject to certain restrictions on the assets side of their business, but these restrictions are imposed on them not by the provisions of the Banking Act but rather by the respective *Land* legislation. They are prohibited from involvement in certain speculative transactions, such as trade in shares, unless specifically authorised to do so by the supreme *Land* supervisory authority. Competition among the public savings banks is limited by the principle of regional exclusivity, under which a savings bank's geographic area of operations is basically identical with that of its guarantor.

At the end of 1989, the savings bank sector encompassed 10 regional giro institutions (including the Sparkasse der Stadt Berlin-West (Savings Bank of the City of West Berlin) and the Deutsche Girozentrale – Deutsche Kommunalbank (DGZ), Frankfurt/Berlin), all of which act as the savings banks' liquidity collection points and provide them with the means of both obtaining refinancing at all times and co-operating in syndicated lending, in trade in shares and in external business. Since the 1960s, they have increasingly engaged in large-scale industrial loan business, local authority loan business, mortgage business and in foreign business. They also have integrated mortgage business departments as well as building and loan associations of their own. This has led to fiercer competition not only among these regional giro institutions but also with larger savings banks. As the *Landesbanken*, the regional giro institutions are also the principal bankers of the *Länder* governments. They are public law entities, the liabilities of which are guaranteed by the respective *Länder* governments and/or the regional associations of the savings banks.

The larger regional giro institutions are universal banks that operate on a global scale and maintain branch offices, subsidiary banks and representative offices abroad. The five largest are the Westdeutsche Landesbank of Düsseldorf/Münster, the Bayerische Landesbank Girozentrale in Munich, the Norddeutsche Landesbank Girozentrale of Hannover/Braunschweig, the Hessische Landesbank Girozentrale in Frankfurt am Main and (as a result of a merger) the Südwestdeutsche Landesbank Girozentrale in Stuttgart/Mannheim. The Deutsche Girozentrale at the top of the savings bank sector, which conducts large loan and issue business of its own, only ranks ninth.

Credit co-operatives

Over the past decades, the category of banks encompassing the credit co-operatives has increased its market share from about one-tenth to 16.5%. At the same time, the total number of credit co-operatives declined to 3223 at the end of 1989, and thus to one quarter of that recorded some 30 years earlier, while the number of banking outlets increased slightly to 15 789. Credit co-operatives date back more than 125 years, when the idea of 'helping members to help themselves' was developed by Hermann Schulze-Delitzsch for the small business sector, and by Friedrich Wilhelm Raiffeisen for the agricultural sector. Today, total membership in credit co-operatives exceeds 11 million, of which some 60% are wage and salary earners. Since the amendment of the *Genossenschaftsgesetz* (Co-operative Bank Act), credit co-operatives have been permitted to conduct business with non-members, subject to that being provided for in the by-laws of the respective credit co-operative or people's bank involved. Basically, the co-operative banking sector has a three-tier structure, the lowest being marked by the individual credit co-operatives.

The regional institutions of the credit co-operatives are interlinked in a network at regional level. The number of such institutions has dropped drastically to only three, lately mainly as a result of their being incorporated into the Deutsche Genossenschaftsbank (DG Bank) in Frankfurt am Main, rather than through mergers between individual regional institutions. In Bavaria, as in Berlin even earlier, the individual credit co-operatives are directly affiliated to the DG Bank, but the trend towards a two-tier structure has not continued in more recent times.

The above concept is opposed most strongly by the Südwestdeutsche Genossenschaftszentralbank in Frankfurt am Main and by the Westdeutsche Genossenschafts-Zentralbank in Düsseldorf. Moreover, in connection with a necessary major increase in capital recently, the Board of the DG Bank was incapable of preventing the remaining regional institutions of the credit co-operatives from acquiring direct stakes in some of those regional institutions that are incorporated into its network, even though it would have preferred a holding company concept.

The DG Bank, the consolidated balance sheet total of which came to some DM 187 billion at the end of 1989, is a public law entity with the statutory task of fostering the German credit co-operative sector. It is a universal and internationally operating bank with the right to issue bonds. At the end of 1989, two-thirds of its capital was held by the regional institutions of the credit co-operatives, while a quarter was held by other co-operative institutions and very minor stakes by the federal and *Länder* governments. Key roles in the network are played by the Schwäbisch Hall building and loan association and by the RV insurance company. Together with the central institutions of the credit co-operative sectors in France (Caisse Nationale de Crédit Agricole), in the Netherlands

(Rabobank), in Belgium (CERA Spaarbank), in Austria (Raiffeisen-Zentralbank) and in Finland (Okobank), the DG Bank has joined the Unico-Banking Group to give its private and corporate clients access to the whole range of services offered by all 37 000 local credit co-operatives in these countries.

Mortgage banks

The business operations of specialised banks are very heterogeneous in character. A clearly demarcated category is that of the mortgage banks, which encompasses 28 private law mortgage and ship mortgage banks (established in the form of public limited companies) as well as 9 public law mortgage banks. The latter group also includes *Landschaften*, *Ritterschaften*, the *Wohnungsbaukreditanstalten* (housing credit institutions) of four *Länder* governments and the (now privatised and incorporated) Deutsche Pfandbriefanstalt, formerly a governmental housing policy body. By tradition, mortgage banks grant senior long term mortgages and obtain refinancing through the issue of mortgage bonds and through wholesale deposits with financial intermediaries. In addition, most mortgage banks provide loans to municipal and local authorities against the issue of communal bonds. In the case of many institutions, the volume of their local authority loan business now exceeds that of their housing mortgage business.

The private law institutions are governed by the strict provisions of the *Hypothekenbankgesetz* (Mortgage Bank Act) or the *Schiffsbankgesetz* (Ship Mortgage Bank Act), while the public law mortgage banks are subject to the provisions of both the *Pfandbriefgesetz* (Act on Mortgage and Similar Bonds Issued by Public Credit Institutions) and the respective formation acts or by-laws approved by the government. And finally, there are also several banks of the universal type which are likewise engaged in mortgage business and which also have the right to issue mortgage bonds, namely the aforementioned three combined commercial and mortgage banks as well as the regional giro institutions.

Other specialised banks

In addition, the category of specialised banks encompasses 18 private law and 12 public law building and loan associations, 9 of which are in-house departments of other public law credit institutions. Under the provisions of the *Bausparkassengesetz* (Act on Building and Loan Associations), the main task of such associations is the granting of junior mortgage loans to prospective private house-owners and housing construction companies; to a lesser extent, they also grant local authority loans earmarked for particular purposes. They obtain by far most of their refinancing through savings deposits. Together with other funds, these deposits are used to grant loans under savings contracts to savers with building and loan associations. Wholesale deposits, the acceptance of sight and time deposits as well as the issue of bearer bonds are used predominantly to provide advance and interim financing as well as other loans.

The small but significant category of banks with special functions encompasses five public law institutions owned by the federal or *Länder* governments and 11 private law specialised banks. They fulfil sector-specific financial tasks in areas such as export financing, the arrangement of financing for development aid projects, assistance for small and medium-sized businesses and publicly assisted financing for industry, agriculture and housing construction.

One of the largest institutions of this kind is the Kreditanstalt für Wiederaufbau (KfW; the Reconstruction Loan Corporation) in Frankfurt am Main, the total business volume of which came to DM 122 billion at the end of 1989. Its core business is the granting of loans to promote German industry, either in the form of investment loans for small and medium-sized businesses, loans to promote environmental protection and other structural policy measures or in the form of loans to finance exports. Some of the funds needed by the KfW are raised on the capital markets. Others are taken from the European Recovery Programme (ERP) Special Fund. Since 1990, the implementation of special lending programmes to finance the economic reconstruction of the new *Länder* has caused the credit operations of both the KfW and some other public law institutions to take on a completely new order of magnitude. Part of the cost of the low interest loans provided by the KfW for this purpose are borne by the federal government, while the other part reduces its own interest margins. Loans and grants within the scope of financial co-operation with developing countries, the KfW's second field of activity, are financed through funds appropriated in the federal budget. The Deutsche Pfandbrief- und Hypothekenbank AG in Wiesbaden (formerly, up to November 1989, the Deutsche Pfandbriefanstalt, a public law entity), which has a consolidated balance sheet total of DM 70 billion, has meanwhile been partially privatised.

Further large banks with special functions are, among others, the AKA Ausfuhrkredit-GmbH, the Deutsche Verkehrs-Bank AG, the IKB Deutsche Industriebank AG, the Liquiditäts-Konsortialbank, the Deutsche Ausgleichsbank, the Landwirtschaftliche Rentenbank and (since 1 July 1991) the Staatsbank Berlin.

A significant role in both payment and saving operations is played by the two postal savings bank offices and the thirteen postal giro offices, all of which are legally subordinate to the Deutsche Bundespost (Federal Post Office) and have been incorporated, since Bundespost reorganisation in 1989, into the Deutsche Bundespost POSTBANK. At the end of 1989, the postal giro and postal savings bank offices carried some 22 million savings accounts plus just under 5 million postal giro accounts with a total balance of DM 61 billion, which could be disposed of at almost 18 000 post offices. The funds deposited are largely used to finance the Bundespost's capital spending.

Not included in the Monthly Balance Sheet Statistics at the end of 1989 were 51 investment companies, the Deutsche Kassenverein AG (the central securities depository which was established through the merger of six regional securities depositories at the end of 1989) and the Deutsche Auslandskassenverein as well as 28 guarantee banks and other credit institutions.

Associations of the banking sector and their members

The five associations mentioned first are also members of the Zentraler Kreditausschuß (Central Credit Committee):

Bundesverband deutscher Banken eV (BdB)
(Federal Association of German Banks)
Mohrenstrasse 35–41
D–53173 Bonn
Tel: (0228) 16630
Members: big banks, regional and other commercial banks, private bankers, private law mortgage banks, private law banks with special functions, branches of foreign banks.

Deutscher Sparkassen- und Giroverband eV (DSGV)
(German Savings Banks and Giro Association)
Simrockstrasse 4
D–53113 Bonn
Tel: (0228) 2040
Members: savings banks, Landesbanken/regional giro institutions.

Verband der Deutschen Freien Öffentlichen Sparkassen eV
(Association of German Independent Public Savings Banks)
Central Office
Am Brill 1
D–28195 Bremen
Members: independent savings banks.

Bundesverband der Deutschen Volksbanken und Raiffeisenbanken eV (BVR)
(Federal Association of German People's Banks and Raiffeisen Banks)
Heussallee 5
D–53113 Bonn
Tel: (0228) 5090
Members: credit co-operatives, regional institutions of the credit co-operatives.

Verband öffentlicher Banken eV
(Association of Public Banks)
Godesberger Allee 88
D–53175 Bonn
Tel: (0228) 81920
Members: public law mortgage banks, public law banks with special functions, Landesbanken/regional giro institutions.

Verband deutscher Hypothekenbanken eV
(Association of German Mortgage Banks)
Holbeinstrasse 17
D–53175 Bonn
Tel: (0228) 372026
Members: private law mortgage banks.

Verband der Privaten Bausparkassen eV
(Association of Private Building and Loan Associations)
Dottendorfer Strasse 82
D–53129 Bonn
Members: private law building and loan associations.

Bundesgeschäftsstelle der Landesbausparkassen im Deutschen Sparkassen- und Giroverband eV
(Federal Office of the *Länder* Building and Loan Associations in the German Savings Banks and Giro Association)

Simrockstrasse 4
D–53113 Bonn
Members: *Länder* building and loan associations.

Verband der Auslandsbanken in Deutschland eV (Association of Foreign Banks in Germany)
Schaumainkai 45
D–60596 Frankfurt am Main
Tel: (069) 627330
Members: subsidiaries and branches of foreign banks.

Vereinigung der Repräsentanten ausländischer Banken in der Bundesrepublik Deutschland eV
(Association of Representatives of Foreign Banks in the Federal Republic of Germany)
PO Box 102341
D–60000 Frankfurt am Main
Tel: (069) 294039

Bundesverband Deutscher Leasing-Gesellschaften eV (Federal Association of German Leasing Companies)
Heilsbachstrasse 32
D–53123 Bonn
Tel: (0228) 641033

Deutscher Factoring-Verband eV
(Association of German Factoring Companies)
Frankfurt am Main
Office of the Management:
Rheinallee 3d
D–55116 Mainz
Tel: (06131) 232867-69

Gesamtverband der Wohnungswirtschaft eV (GdW)
(Central Association of the Housing Industry)
Bismarckstrasse 7
D–50672 Cologne

Bundesverband Deutscher Investmentgesellschaften eV (BVI)
(Federal Association of German Investment Companies)
Eschenheimer Anlage 28
D–60318 Frankfurt am Main

Appendix: Structure of the banking system in the former GDR

In contrast to the Deutsche Bundesbank, the Staatsbank of the former GDR was totally dependent on instructions from the government. Under the provisions of the *Gesetz über die Staatsbank* (Staatsbank Act) of 1974, it was the GDR Council of Ministers' central body for the implementation of the monetary and credit policies adopted by the Party and the government. It was the central bank as well as a commercial bank with 220 branch offices conducting business with the industrial, construction, domestic distribution and transport sectors as well as with the post and telecommunications industry. It had the exclusive right to issue banknotes and coins, determined the accounting rates used in foreign trade and payments, acted as the government's cash office, compiled statements on the credit positions of the sectors under its jurisdiction, monitored the fulfilment of the plan and fixed the rates of interest on both loans and savings. It determined deviations from the basic interest rate of 5% on scheduled loans, either upward as interest on arrears in the event of plan parameters not being met, or downward for investment deemed to be of particular macroeconomic benefit.

However, a number of financial functions were excluded from the Staatsbank's area of operations and handled by legally independent institutions. The Deutsche Außenhandelsbank (DABA), for instance, was entrusted with the financial settlement of foreign trade transactions, and particluarly those with other socialist countries. The Deutsche Handelsbank AG was responsible for business with non-socialist economies, and thus also acted as a clearing bank in intra-German trade. The activities of both the Bank für Landwirtschaft und Nahrungsgüterwirtschaft and the 96 Genossenschaftskassen für Handwerk und

Gewerbe were restricted to specific sectors, the former to business with agriculture and the latter to that with the crafts and small business.

The 196 savings banks – municipal and district council institutions – played a key role as financial intermediaries. At the end of 1989, they accounted for about four-fifths of the total balance of GDR Mark 162 billion on all individuals' giro and savings accounts. The remainder was accounted for by the aforementioned institutions as well as by the postal savings bank and postal giro offices as well as by the Reichsbahnkasse and the Reichsbahnsparkasse, all of which were subject to supervision by the Staatsbank. The interest paid on savings was 3.25% in all cases. Most of the savings accumulated at the savings banks were made available to the government, or to state-owned enterprises and co-operatives, via the Staatsbank, in principle at a fixed interest rate of 4%. Direct loans to craftsmen, small businesses and local utilities, consumer credit for certain accepted purposes and building loans for individuals were of only very minor significance.

The first half of 1990, i.e. the period prior to the entry into force of the *Vertrag über die Schaffung einer Währungs-, Wirtschafts- und Sozialunion zwischen der Bundesrepublik Deutschland und der Deutschen Demokratischen Republik* (Treaty Establishing a Monetary, Economic and Social Union between the Federal Republic of Germany and the German Democratic Republic), saw the implementation of first measures to reform the banking system. At the beginning of 1990, GDR citizens were given the opportunity of opening interest-bearing Deutsche Mark accounts with the Staatsbank, the balances of which could be freely disposed of. On the basis of an *Änderungsgesetz zum Staatsbankgesetz* (Act to Amend the Staatsbank Act), the Staatsbank transferred all its loans, including those for housing in the GDR, as well as a major proportion of its equipment and staff, to a newly established subsidiary, the Deutsche Kreditbank AG (DKB), with effect from 1 April

1990. This marked the first step towards a separation of functions along the road to a market economy banking system. Formally, the Staatsbank was also made independent of instructions from the government.

It was only after the entry into force of the monetary union, i.e. upon the introduction of the Deutsche Mark in the GDR on 1 July 1990, and the general licensing of West German and foreign credit institutions to conduct banking business there, that the process of restoring responsibility for credit and deposit policies to the individual institutions entered into a decisive phase. That date also saw the entry into force in full of the Banking Act of the Federal Republic of Germany. The Deutsche Bank and the Dresdner Bank were particularly quick off the mark; they established subsidiaries together with the DKB, and were thus able – albeit indirectly to begin with – to take over a significant proportion of the buildings and staff of the Staatsbank or the DKB. Other banks, by contrast, had to rely on their own resources when building up country-wide branch networks or selected establishments.

Particularly intense efforts to develop the savings banks and credit co-operatives in the former GDR into market economy-oriented universal banks were undertaken both by the West German savings bank sector under the lead of the DSGV and the DGZ and by the West German credit co-operative sector under the lead of the BVR and the DG Bank. What proved to be particularly efficient in this context was the adoption of sponsoring concepts to train banking personnel and introduce modern technology. The partial withdrawal, in an orderly manner, of the old institutions' deposits with the Staatsbank necessitated special arrangements for the refinancing of the Staatsbank on the interbank market and extensive bond issues by the Staatsbank on the German capital market.

However, the entry into force of the monetary union on 1 July 1990 resulted in the Staatsbank losing all the functions of both a bank of issue and a central bank. Since then, these functions have been performed by the Deutsche Bundesbank, which initially established 15 branch offices of its own in the territory of the former GDR as well as a Provisional Administrative Office in East Berlin. The Provisional Administrative Office ceased to function with effect from 1 November 1992, and became the nucleus of the new Land Central Bank of the Free State of Saxonia and Thuringia, i.e. a main office of the Deutsche Bundesbank, to which all branches within that new constituency must report direct. Brandenburg and East Berlin joined the former Land Central Bank of Berlin, while Mecklenburg-Western Pomerania, together with Schleswig-Holstein and Hamburg, formed another new Land Central Bank with its headquarters in Hamburg. And finally, Saxony-Anhalt joined forces with Bremen and Lower Saxony.

2 France

General outline

The French financial system was subject to rapid and far-reaching change in the 1980s. In view of the globalisation of markets and technology-related financial innovations, the authorities have seen themselves compelled, particularly since 1985, to create nationally and internationally competitive banking structures. La Nouvelle Loi Bancaire de 1984, *the comprehensive reform of French banking legislation at the beginning of 1984, as well as a great number of other legislative and administrative measures, helped to open up existing and develop new financial markets, increased competition among credit institutions and ultimately developed Paris into a financial centre of international standing.*

The rapid growth of the capital markets, the newly created market for billets de trésorerie *(commercial paper floated by non-banks) and the increased self-financing powers of enterprises led to a certain process of disintermediation in the 1980s. At the end of 1989, only 62% of all lendings in the economy as a whole were accounted for by credit institutions, as against 79% in 1979. The credit institutions responded to this trend by increasingly diversifying their financial services. They expanded their financial credit and leasing business significantly. They increased their activities on the money and capital markets, either on their own account through the issue of certificates of deposit, through the building-up of larger trading portfolios of securities and through arbitrage transactions within the scope of an active management of their own assets and liabilities, or indirectly through the management of the securities portfolios and other assets of* Organismes de Placement Collectif en Valeurs Mobilières *(OPCVM; investment funds). All financial services that allowed fees to be earned were promoted, namely advisory services for and support of enterprises in cases of mergers and acquisitions of participating interests, a field previously reserved for* banques d'affaires *(investment banks). Innovative instruments for enterprises' risk management (currency and interest swaps, options, etc) and a broad range of possibilities for the long term investment of private clients' savings, such as investment fund units, life insurance and old-age pension schemes, were also promoted.*

In structural terms, comprehensive diversification was accompanied by respecialisation within larger banking groups, either through the establishment of securities houses and life insurance companies, or through the acquisition of controlling interests in existing institutions such as leasing companies and, since 1988, stock trading companies. The closer ties to the insurance sector are documented by a great number of co-operation agreements on the marketing of insurance policies, and by the establishment of reciprocal capital links between banks and insurance companies (as were agreed between the Banque Nationale de Paris (BNP) and the Union des Assurances de Paris (UAP) in March 1989).

The official policy of deregulation, especially the abolition of the age-old practice of imposing credit ceilings, has led to an exemplary increase in competition between banks. This increase also owes something to the sharp drop in lending at special terms and conditions and to the standardisation of savings business products. Inevitable consequences thereof, however, included mergers within the banking sector and the growing propensity of banks to acquire participating interests in insurance companies and other non-banks. Since 1985, there has also been a remarkable acceleration of the internationalisation of the French banking system. In anticipation of Europe 1992, the last capital controls were abolished at the beginning of 1990.

Role of the Banque de France

Key changes to monetary policy were effected as early as 1987. The use of quantitative credit controls as an instrument for the direct management of money stock was revoked. Since then, increased use has been made of the instrument of interest rate management via interventions on the money market. Interest rate policy is supplemented by minimum reserve requirements and interventions on the exchange market. Since December 1986, the Banque de France, as the competent institution, has been offering *pensions surappels d'offres* (sale and repurchase agreements) under a tender procedure at short intervals, with the central bank itself not only deciding when to initiate such transactions but also fixing the maturity in each case. The Banque de France uses the tender bids as a basis for determining a single interest rate (the tender rate) and the total volume of bids to be accepted. The ceiling on the very short term interbank rates is marked by the rate fixed for sale and repurchase agreements with maturities of five to ten days, concluded upon the initiative of the banks involved. That rate is usually up to three-quarters of one per cent higher than the tender rate, and is of significance to banks only in the event of sudden liquidity bottlenecks.

However, the central bank may also conclude sale and repurchase agreements at the current market rate, or conduct direct open market operations by buying or selling treasury bills or other money market paper issued by the credit institutions. At the end of 1989, i.e. after the change of October that year, the minimum reserve requirements, used to influence bank liquidity on the basis of changes in the credit institutions' deposits, were 5.5% for sight deposits and 3% for all other liabilities of residents subject to them. In January 1990, the scope of the minimum reserve requirements was extended further to encompass residents' foreign currency liabilities, including certificates of deposit and other bank debt certificates with original maturities of less than two years. October 1990, December 1991 and, finally, May 1992 all saw significant cuts in the minimum reserve requirements, so that money market rates have become more volatile. Since 16 May 1992, the minimum reserve ratios on French franc deposits have been 1% for sight deposits, 1% for savings accounts and 0.5% for time deposits with maturities of one year or less.

The ultimate goal of French monetary policy is to ensure the internal and external stability of the currency not only by limiting the growth of both the monetary aggregates and the volume of credit, but also by defending the parity of the French franc within the European Monetary System (EMS). Where the various aggregates are concerned, key importance was attached to limiting the expansion of the money stock (initially M2, but later M3) by fixing an annual target corridor. The defence of the French currency's exchange rate *vis-à-vis* the Deutsche Mark, which has in fact assumed the function of the stability anchor in the EMS (the most recent downwards valuation of the French franc's bilateral central rate against the Deutsche Mark was at the beginning of 1987), as well as the increasing consistency, since 1983, of the French monetary authorities' pursuit of an anti-inflation policy, have led to the levels of both short and long term interest rates in France being only marginally higher than those in Germany. The turbulences involving the EMS currencies in September 1992 and July/August 1993 brought no change in the central rate of the French franc *vis-à-vis* the Deutsche Mark. In August 1993, however, the margin of fluctuation in the ERM was widened from $\pm 2^1/_4\%$ to $\pm 15\%$.

The gap between the inflation rates recorded in the two countries has meanwhile been closed through convergence on the traditionally more stable Deutsche Mark. For some time now, the German rate of inflation has actually been slightly higher than that of France and a number of other core countries in the EU. Doubts of market participants as to whether the current situation will continue to prevail for a longer period are reflected by, among other things, the fact that real interest rates, i.e. the nominal interest rates adjusted for inflation, are still lower in Germany than in France (and in other EU member countries).

Although the Banque de France is the institution primarily responsible for implementing monetary policy, it has always – since 1945 – had to confer with the minister of finance on key issues. In cases of conflict, the minister of finance had the right to issue instructions to the central bank, and there was also the possibility of the governor of the central bank being removed from office. In line with the provisions of the Maastricht Treaty, which require central banks to be made more independent of their respective ministries of finance before entry into the third stage of the Economic and Monetary Union, the position of the Banque de France was strengthened by appropriate legislation as early as August 1993 (Law No. 93-980 of 4 August 1993, as amended by Law No. 93-1444 of 31 December 1993). The autonomous Conseil de la Politique Monétaire (Monetary Policy Council) is responsible for formulating and implementing monetary policy. The prime minister and the minister of finance both have the right to attend and submit proposals at its meetings, but they have no vote. Six of the nine members of the Council are elected by the Conseil des Ministres (Council of Ministers), while the governor of the Banque de France and his two deputies are members by virtue of the offices they hold. The law stipulates expressly that price stability is the final goal of monetary policy, although the Banque de France is required to perform its tasks within the framework of the government's general economic policy. The Council is prohibited from accepting instructions from the government. On 27 January 1994, the Council decided that inflation should not exceed 2%. Two intermediate objectives were adopted: firstly, the external objective of stabilising the currency's external value in line with the decision of the EU Council of Ministers and central bank governors of 2 August 1993 to uphold the parity grid of the exchange rate mechanism, and secondly, the internal medium term objective in respect of the M3 aggregate, the expansion of which must no longer be in line with an annual target, but rather tend – over the medium term – to be in the range of 5%. The other activities of the Banque de France are entrusted to its General Council, which consists of the members of the Monetary Policy Council plus an elected representative of the staff and an auditor representing the government. For purposes of carrying out the manifold tasks it has over and beyond its responsibility for monetary policy, tasks ranging from the issue of banknotes and involvement in payments to banking supervision, the Banque de France has a network of some 200 branch offices at its disposal.

Legislation and banking supervision

Another key task of the central bank is that of banking supervision. Formally responsible is the Commission

Bancaire (Banking Commission), which is chaired by the governor of the central bank. Its other members are the Directeur du Trésor (head of the State Treasury) in the Ministry of Economics and Finance, the president of the financial division of the Conseil d'Etat (supreme administrative court), a member of the Cour de Cassation (Court of Cassation, i.e. the court of final appeal in France) and one representative each of management and labour in the banking sector. The operational staff required is largely provided by the Banque de France. The Banking Commission's main task is to monitor whether banking legislation and all banking supervision rules are adhered to, and it has the right to take disciplinary action. The Commission is assisted by the Comité de la Reglementation Bancaire (Committee on Banking Rules), which is chaired by the Minister of Economics and Finance and in which the governor of the central bank and four other members have seats. The Committee is responsible for defining all general supervisory rules applicable to credit institutions. A third body, the Comité des Etablissements de Crédit (Committee on Credit Institutions), which is chaired by the Directeur du Trésor and has two other members, takes individual supervisory decisions on the basis of banking legislation and the supervisory rules.

The *Loi Bancaire* (Banking Act) of 1984 finally did away with the previously applicable principle of specialisation, which had governed the Banking Act of 1941 and which had only been given up in part in the course of its revision in 1967. At the time, a distinction had still been made between *banques de dépôts* (depository institutions), *banques d'affaires* (investment banks) and banks for medium to long term loans. In addition, there was a great number of other financial institutions subject to different supervisory regulations. The Act of 1984 is based on the term *établissement de crédit* (credit institution), which covers not only all banks, credit co-operatives and savings banks, without distinguishing between them, but also non-bank financial institutions and specialised financial institutions. The now newly defined category of market institutions, which comprises so-called market banks and securities houses, is likewise subject to banking supervision (see Appendix 2).

For purposes of limiting the credit risks, all the credit institutions covered by the Banking Act were required, on a consolidated basis, to meet a solvency ratio of 5%, i.e. the appropriately weighted credit risks must be covered by at least 5% own funds. In line with EU requirements, this level has now been raised to a minimum of 8%. Liabilities on call at any time must be covered in full (100%) by liquid assets, with the likelihood of such liabilities actually being called, or the cover actually becoming necessary, rather than legal criteria playing the significant part since 1988. At least 60% of all long term domestic currency loans must be covered by capital or appropriate long term funds. Since 1989, the global currency risk has been limited to 40% (and open positions in respect of an individual currency to 15%) of the capital. Where other market risks that may arise in conjunction with, above all, forward contract and securities positions are concerned, special accounting and reporting requirements were initially adopted in 1988 and 1989.

Market shares of the individual categories of banks

The French banking system has been relatively compact for quite some time, and the trend towards a concentration within the categories of banks is continuing in many areas, despite the legal separation of certain special transactions (see Table 2). At the end of 1989, banking supervision covered a total of 2085 credit institutions which maintained a network of 25 284 regular branch offices in France. Just over half of all banking transactions were executed by members of the Association Française des Banques (AFB;

Table 2 *Market shares of French credit institutions[1,2] (at the end of 1989)*

A. Broken down by legal category (legal form of establishment)

	Loans	Deposits	Business volume Total	Business volume Net[2]
	in %	in %	in %	in FF billion
Banques AFB	50.2	51.2	55.2	7 153
Banques mutualistes ou coopératives	21.6	27.8	16.3	2 118
Caisses d'épargne	4.2	15.6	8.0	1 037
Caisses de crédit municipal	0.3	0.2	0.2	21
Sociétes financières (SF)	7.3	3.8	11.2	1 456
Institutions financières spécialisées (IFS)	16.4	1.3	8.6	1 116
Maisons de titres	0.0	0.1	0.5	69
Total funds				
in %	100	100	100	–
in FF billion	5 190	4 170	–	12 970

B. Broken down by homogeneous category of institutions

Credit institutions or linking systems with a general business orientation[3]				
– Very large	*49.9*	*72.2*	*50.7*	*6 577*
– Large	*5.6*	*6.4*	*5.5*	*713*
– Small and medium-sized	*1.8*	*2.2*	*1.3*	*174*
Local banks	*1.7*	*2.1*	*1.6*	*211*
Specialised financial institutions	*29.9*	*4.7*	*20.4*	*2 643*
Market institutions	*0.4*	*1.3*	*2.7*	*347*
Various specialised institutions[4]	*6.9*	*8.1*	*9.6*	*1 242*
Foreign banks	*3.2*	*2.5*	*7.8*	*1 013*
Other credit institutions	*0.6*	*0.5*	*0.4*	*50*

Source: Commission Bancaire, Rapport *1989*

1 Etablissements de crédit *and* maisons de titres, *including their branches abroad, which are subject to banking supervision in France.*

2 Adjusted for interbank relations in France and abroad, including relations to affiliated banks.

3 A vocation générale.

4 Etablissements de groupe d'ingénerie ou de portefeuille.

French Banking Association), i.e. by those collectively known as the AFB banks. Almost 50% of all loans granted, 55% of the deposits carried and 43% of the total business volume being accounted for by the three largest banks: Banque Nationale de Paris (BNP), Crédit Lyonnais and Société Générale. Although all three of these banks were nationalised after the Second World War (as were 41 additional institutions with total assets of more than FF 1 billion in another wave of general nationalisation in 1982), Société Générale is one of the seven banks returned to private ownership by the Conservative government under Prime Minister Chirac between November 1986 and February 1988, followed later by the BNP.

Credit institutions and linking systems with a general business orientation

The category of so-called AFB banks also includes former investment banks, such as the Compagnie Financière de Suez. The AFB banks are all deemed to be universal banks, but their geographic distribution is the factor deciding whether they are classified, under the new breakdown, as 'very large' credit institutions (which operate nationwide), as 'large' credit institutions (which, although not operating nationwide, are represented in several regions; included are 11 individual banks and the linking system of Crédit Coopératif) or as 'small and medium-sized' credit institutions or linking systems with a general business orientation (which are represented in one or two regions; included are 22 individual AFB banks as well as the system of the municipal cash offices).

The first category of very large credit institutions or linking systems comprises not only the three banks mentioned earlier but also four linking systems that operate throughout France: Crédit Agricole, Caisses d'Epargne,

Crédit Populaire and Crédit Mutuel. By far the most significant of these is Crédit Agricole, which had a total business volume of FF 1379 billion at the end of 1989, the equivalent of a good tenth of the total business volume of all credit institutions. In addition to the central institution, the linking system Caisse Nationale de Crédit Agricole (CNCA), includes 122 affiliated institutions, comprising 91 regional cash offices, 18 other *sociétés de financement* (SOFI; finance companies) which provide small and medium-sized enterprises in the agricultural sector with equity capital, and 13 institutions which act as guarantors for certain loans (UNICEF). Some 73 000 persons are employed by the central institution in approximately 10 000 branches, 5638 of which are permanent offices. Most of the system's clients – small businesses and individuals – are active in the agricultural sector, but a growing number now also come from other sectors.

The savings banks, which are owned by local authorities and which formerly conducted almost exclusively savings deposit business, with the funds involved traditionally being passed on to the public Caisse des Dépôts et Consignations for investment, have been in the midst of a process of transformation for years. Since 1987, the savings banks have been permitted, within certain limits, to grant loans to companies. Whereas the number of branch offices rose slightly to 4322 in 1989, the number of institutions dropped by 77 to 224. The market share of savings banks totalled only 8%, but their share in deposit business, which is largely accounted for by tax-free savings deposits of the type *Livret A*, came to almost 16%. At the top of the linking system is the Centre National des Caisses d'Epargne et de Prévoyance (CENCEP), which – given the forthcoming single European market – pursues a policy of co-operation with other savings bank organisations in Europe. The savings banks also compete with the Caisse d'Epargne, the national postal savings bank, which has some 17 000 post offices at its disposal as outlets. Although postal savings and postal giro deposits, as well as the significant direct deposits at the Treasury Department of the Ministry of Finance are not subject to banking supervision, they are included – in line with their respective degree of liquidity – in the appropriate monetary aggregates of the Banque de France.

The 33 *banques populaires* (peoples' banks or credit co-operatives), with some 1600 branch offices and a balance sheet total of FF 337 billion, form a major separate linking system. Their clients are primarily small and medium-size businesses, craftsmen and self-employed people in cities and towns. It is not necessary to be a member of a credit co-operative to obtain a loan.

The fourth linking system of country-wide significance is that recently formed by the 23 institutions of Crédit Mutuel, all of which are members of the Confédération Nationale du Crédit Mutuel, and the 10 cash offices of Crédit Mutuel Agricole et Rural. The system's total business volume came to FF 327 billion at the end of 1989. Despite considerable diversification, some 5000 branches, of which 3609 are permanent offices, ensure that the system's core business is still savings. The system is represented primarily in Alsace, Lorraine and Brittany.

Of rather more regional significance are eleven AFB banks and the system of Crédit Coopératif with a business volume of FF 713 billion. Within their areas of operation, the 11 regional banks are well represented by 1882 branch offices. At FF 49 billion, on average, the balance sheet totals of the individual institutions far exceed the national average. External operations and foreign currency business play a major role, although not to the same extent, in relative terms, as in the case of the three 'very large' banks.

Specialised financial institutions

The category of universal banks must be distinguished from that of specialised institutions, which can be broken down into two sub-categories. By far the most important sub-category encompasses a total of 816 specialised financial institutions, of which 62 are AFB banks, 726 are financing companies and 28 are other specialised financial institutions. They are all institutions which concentrate on certain financial transactions with specific types of clients on grounds relating either to their legal form of establishment or to an appropriate government mandate, or which have decided to specialise in such a manner on strategic considerations. Their market share amounts to about a fifth, or a third, if all specialised institutions are taken together. Their share in lending business comes to about 30% (nearer 40% if all specialised institutions are taken as a whole). The volume of deposits from corporate clients and individuals at the disposal of these institutions for refinancing purposes is not very large. Equity capital and revenue bonds account for 34% of their funding basis, and funds from other credit institutions, above all from AFB banks, for some 47%. In particular, the institutions involved finance the acquisition of housing, provide commercial real estate loans or loans for other private purposes, lend funds to the self-employed and small and medium-size businesses, finance the energy sector or energy conservation measures and, finally, deal in loan guarantees (usually for members of the *sociétés de caution mutuelle*, or reciprocal guarantee schemes). The best known of the *institutions financières spécialisées* are institutions such as Caisse Centrale de Coopération (CCCE), Comptoir des Entrepreneurs, Crédit d'Equipement des PME (CEPME), Crédit Foncier de France, the industrial development bank Crédit National, regional development companies (SDR) and, finally, SOFARIS which provides venture capital. Banque Française du Commerce Extérieur (BFCE), which was nationalised in 1946, is an AFB bank which specialises in the financing of imports and exports and which co-operates with Compagnie Française d'Assurance pour le Commerce Extérieur (COFACE) on behalf of the government.

Market institutions

A new category comprising a growing number of institutions is that formed by what are known as *établissements de marché* (market institutions), which includes 27 *banques de marché* (market banks) of often considerable size and 139 *maisons de titres* (securities houses). A further 22 banks and finance companies, which are owned by and largely operate for industrial enterprises and insurance companies, are also included in the category of 'various specialised institutions'. Although the institutions operate independently, they frequently have capital links to industrial enterprises or to major banks and insurance companies. About a quarter of the *maisons de titres* are under foreign control. Their market significance is far greater than that reflected in their business volume of FF 347 billion (at the end of 1989). These institutions, most of which have their headquarters and only a single office in Paris, concentrate on interbank business and on securities transactions on the money and capital markets. They are also highly active in the field of off-balance sheet-transactions. They conduct business for their own account and for the account of banks and investment funds. They are subject to banking supervision.

Banks' international links

The internationalisation of the French banking sector has increased considerably in recent years. At the end of 1989, some FF 2370 billion, or 20%, of all bank liabilities in France (excluding those of branches abroad) were denominated in foreign currencies, with FF 482 billion of that total being accounted for by liabilities *vis-à-vis* residents (of which FF 112 billion were liabilities on resident non-banks). The capital of more than 250 institutions was under foreign control, 135 of which are deemed to be foreign banks. On average, every foreign bank (branch or subsidiary) has three outlets. Viewed in terms of overall business volume, their market share came to 7.8%. Where lending and deposit business is concerned, their market share is far smaller because the institutions involved obtain a large proportion of their refinancing on the (national and international) interbank markets, and because they also prefer money market operations on the assets side and deal intensively in off-balance sheet transactions. If solely the AFB banks are considered, the share of foreign institutions in the overall business volume amounted to a fifth, in market transactions to more than a quarter, and that in lending to as much as 12%. Two of the ten largest AFB banks now are Japanese.

Conversely, the larger French banks have established strong positions in financial centres abroad. Nearly 300 foreign branches have a total business volume of FF 1620 billion. At the end of 1989, the aggregate share of French banks in international banking business at home and abroad (including all cross-border transactions, irrespective of the currency involved, as well as all foreign currency transactions with residents) came to about 9% of all the transactions recorded in the statistics of the Bank for International Settlements (BIS) in Basle. The French banks thus ranked third behind the leading banks from Japan and the United States, still just ahead of the banks from Germany, Switzerland and the United Kingdom.

Investment funds

Investment funds, in the form of *organismes de placement collectif en valeurs mobilières* (OPCVM), are subject not to the supervision of the Commission Bancaire, but rather to that of the Commission des Opérations de Bourse (COB; Stock Exchange Commission). Included are not only self-contained investment funds, but also the Sociétés d'Investissement à Capital Variable (SICAV) and the Fonds

Communs de Placement (FCP). The net assets of the rapidly expanding SICAVs totalled FF 1270 billion at the end of 1989, while those of the FCPs came to as much as FF 433 billion. The short term SICAVs had a market share of 57%, not least on account of money market funds, which are particularly attractive in times of high money market rates and flat yield curves.

Associations of the banking sector and their members

The Banking Act of 1984 provides for a two-tier system of representation in the banking sector. Every credit institution must be a member of a representative organisation, and that, in turn, must be a member of the umbrella organisation for the whole banking sector, the Association Française des Etablissements de Crédit (AFEC). There are two types of representative organisations. On the one hand, there are currently six central organisations that have both representative and controlling functions, namely the Caisse Nationale de Crédit Agricole, the Chambre Syndicale des Banques Populaires, the Confédération Nationale de Crédit Mutuel, the Caisse Nationale du Crédit Mutuel, the Caisse Centrale de Crédit Coopératif, the Fédération Centrale du Crédit Mutuel and, finally, the Centre National des Caisses d'Epargne et de Prévoyance. On the other hand, the AFEC also counts professional organisations, such as the Association Française des Banques (in which all banks are members, with the exception of those with a special legal status), the Association des Sociétés Financières, the Fédération Nationale du Crédit Agricole and the Groupement des Institutions Financières Spécialisées, among its members.

3 *Netherlands*

General outline

Amsterdam and Rotterdam are the key banking centres in the Netherlands. A number of its banking institutions can look back on long traditions. In the wake of increasing integration in Europe, external operations by, and thus the foreign assets of, Dutch banks have recently expanded particularly sharply. Algemene Bank Nederland (ABN) and Amsterdam-Rotterdam Bank (AMRO Bank), the two leading banks, have also attained a certain degree of global significance. Conversely, foreign banks – or rather banks controlled from abroad – have markedly increased their share in domestic banking business. In March 1990, the supervisory boards of ABN and AMRO Bank announced a merger of their respective institutions, which has since largely been completed.

The predominance of banks of the universal type became even more marked during the course of the 1980s. In many cases, specialised institutions – such as mortgage banks or credit institutions engaged in securitised lending, i.e. institutions whose core business is mediation in securities trading at the stock exchange – were taken over by universal banks. The savings banks are in the midst of a process of transformation into full-service universal banks. Mergers are leading to the formation of larger and more effective units. Recently, 'one-stop' financing strategies have begun to play a greater role. Since January 1990, the authorities have no longer opposed mergers of banks and insurance companies right from the outset, even though clearance certificates are still required. In anticipation of that change in policy, VSB, the largest Dutch savings bank group, and AMEV, the third-largest insurance company in the Netherlands, have announced their intention to merge their operations. In line with developments in other countries in Europe, the Dutch banks, too, endeavoured in the 1980s to extend their traditional domestic operations to include high-yielding commission fee business, such as leasing, factoring, real estate transactions, the sale of insurance products and, above all, merchant and investment banking. A certain degree of respecialisation has taken place, in that automobile leasing, factoring, the provision of venture capital and credit card business are preferably executed via subsidiaries of banking groups, which operate as individual profit centres.

Role of the De Nederlandsche Bank

Responsibility for monetary policy in the Netherlands is vested in the De Nederlandsche Bank N V, which was established in 1814 and nationalised in 1948. Traditionally the government's banker and the bank of issue in respect of banknotes, it acts as the bankers' bank, promotes giro transactions and is ultimately responsible for banking supervision. The central bank must consult the banking associations before implementing any monetary policy measures. In the event of differences in opinion, the minister of finance must approve the measures in question, and that approval must be confirmed by parliament within two months. The central bank's monetary policy is aimed at keeping prices stable. Its intermediate targets are the control of the domestic money supply (M2) as well as a stable exchange rate of the Dutch guilder in the EMS, i.e. in practice actually *vis-à-vis* the Deutsche Mark. The most important monetary policy instruments are interest rate policy and interventions.

Legislation and banking supervision

The tasks and intervention possibilities of the De Nederlandsche Bank as the competent banking supervisory authority are set out in the *Wet Toezicht Kredietwezen* (Act on Banking Supervision) of 1979, which is based on a comprehensive definition of a credit institution. Automatically included are all commercial undertakings which accept deposits for periods of up to two years and which grant loans or invest funds for their own accounts, and which thus require a banking licence. In addition, the Act provides for other institutions to be subjected to banking supervision, as currently holds true of the mortgage banks and a number of other capital market institutions. Over the years, legislators have fostered the general trend towards both despecialisation and increased competition between credit institutions.

The central bank is entitled, in consultation with the banking associations, to issue further regulations to limit solvency and liquidity risks. It is intended, within the scope of the harmonisation of banking supervision in the European Union, to include other credit risks that arise from a number of as yet unconsidered off-balance sheet transactions as well as previously neglected market risks in the calculation of the equity capital required. In line with the 1988 Basle Accord, the credit risk on over-the-counter

(OTC) derivatives is already included in required solvency levels, on the basis of credit risk equivalents. On the agenda is also the question as to the extent to which the monitoring, on a consolidated basis, of solvency risks, as introduced in line with the EC Directive on the supervision of credit institutions on a consolidated basis, should be extended to include the holding companies of banks, for instance.

Universal banks

The category of commercial banks, which are today referred to officially as universal banks, have a market share of about two-thirds. At the end of 1989, this category also included the Postbank as part of NMB-Postbank. The banks involved have some 2450 branch offices, excluding the 2700 additional outlets provided by post offices. More than half of the just over 80 universal banks are branches or subsidiaries of banks from abroad. The degree of concentration in this category is nevertheless rather high, because almost three-fifths of the assets of all banks at the end of 1989 were accounted for by only two institutions, namely ABN and AMRO Bank. Although AMRO Bank has attained international stature only recently, ABN has long had an extensive network of more than 250 branches and subsidiaries abroad. In the course of the agreed merger in August 1990, the shareholders of these two institutions exchanged their stock for shares in a new company, ABN AMRO Holding, which, in turn, holds the shares of the still independent banks. Since 1986, the Postbank, which was a wholly-owned government undertaking until its recent merger with the Nederlands Middenstandsbank (NMB), has combined cash as well as postal giro and postal savings bank services under one roof, and increasingly also provides mortgage loans and consumer credit in a move towards a general diversification of its services.

Towards the end of 1990, the NMB-Postbank Groep merged anew, namely with Nationale Nederlanden, the leading Dutch insurance company. Viewed in terms of its assets, the new Internationale Nederland Groep (ING) has become number two in the Dutch banking sector, even overtaking the third-ranking Rabobank.

Rabobank Nederland

Rabobank Nederland with its 900 or so affiliated, originally solely agricultural credit co-operatives is regarded as a single institution. With more than 3000 outlets, Rabobank Nederland is well represented throughout the country, and also compares quite well with the two leading banking groups in terms of both its size and the broad range of financial services offered. However, its core business is still with individuals and small corporate clients, as can be seen from the fact that it accounts for some 45% of all savings deposits and for almost 60% of the loans granted to individual clients. The relative significance of interbank and securities transactions, by contrast, is far smaller.

Savings banks

Despite their rather close-knit network of more than 1000 outlets, the local savings banks play only a secondary role by comparison with both the two leading banking groups and the Rabobank Nederland. Their share in the balance sheet total of all institutions subject to banking supervision at the end of 1989 was below 5%. Until only a few years ago, their lending to private enterprises was subject to strict limitations, so that public bonds and public sector loans, or government-guaranteed loans, continue to account for about two-thirds of their assets.

To a certain extent, however, the savings banks have been able to get around the restrictive lending provisions since as long ago as 1971, when they established the Bank der Bondsspaarbanken, which has the status of a normal commercial or universal bank. 95% of the capital of this bank is held by the savings banks, and the remaining share of 5% by the Westdeutsche Landesbank Girozentrale in Düsseldorf. The process of diversification has meanwhile made so much progress that it is actually no longer possible to regard the savings banks as specialised institutions. Since the beginning of 1990, after an amendment of the banking supervision regulations of the De Nederlandsche Bank (undertaken after consultations with the association of savings banks), the savings banks have been able to conduct the same business in other EU member states that they are entitled to in the Netherlands.

Since as early as 1984, the savings banks have also been able to opt for transitional arrangements that provide for the gradual introduction of banking supervision regulations of the kind applicable to universal banks. At the end of 1989, as many as seven savings banks, which together accounted for almost 80% of the consolidated balance sheet total of all savings banks, had subjected themselves to the transitional arrangements (instead of earlier special regulations). Of great significance is also the process of concentration that has been continuing for years; in the period from the end of 1976 to the end of 1986, the number of savings banks declined from 102 to 62. One of the latest examples of the wave of mergers in this sector has been that between the Nutspaarbank West-Nederland, the fifth-largest savings bank, and the Verenigde Spaarbank, the largest institution of its type. The merged institution will have a market share of more than 34% in the savings bank sector. Institutions which are of more than merely local importance also include the Bondsspaarbank voor Midden Noord en Oost Nederlande as well as the Nutspaarbank te 's-Gravenhage.

Specialised credit institutions

There are also quite significant categories of specialised credit institutions in the Netherlands, although the acquisition of participating interests has caused some of them to come under the influence of universal banks. This holds true, above all, of credit institutions that lend against securities, of stockbrokers who are also entitled both to accept deposits and to grant loans against the collateral of securities. Banking supervision also covers mortgage banks. The most important mortgage bank is Rabohypotheekbank, a wholly-owned subsidiary of Rabobank Nederland. The Westland-Utrecht Hypotheekbank and the Friesch-Groningsche Hypotheekbank, the mortgage banks next in size, are owned by insurance companies, namely Nationale Nederland and AEGON, respectively.

Other capital market institutions

The key institution included in the category of 'other capital market institutions' is the Bank voor Nederlandsche Gemeenten, the capital of which is held in equal shares by the central government and the local authorities. It is the fourth-largest bank in the Netherlands. It grants competitive local authority loans, and refinances itself on the capital market. The Nationale Investeringsbank, in which the government has a stake of 50.3%, grants medium and long term investment loans to industry, including publicly guaranteed loans to undertakings facing payment difficulties. This bank is entitled to grant subordinate credit as substitute capital for certain enterprises. Recently, it has also conducted merchant bank business. It has a wholly-owned subsidiary, the Nederlandse Investeringsbank voor Ontwikkelingslanden, which grants credit to developing countries. And finally, it has participating interests in the Export-Financierings-Maatschappij, the Nederlandse Credietverzekering Maatschappij and the Nederlandse Participatie Maatschappij.

Associations of the banking sector and their members

The obligation of the De Nederlandsche Bank to consult the associations of the banking sectors in matters involving monetary policy and banking supervision gives them a special role. The universal banks are members of the Nederlandse Bankiersvereniging (Netherlands Bankers' Association). Rabobank Nederland has transferred certain responsibilities to the banking supervisory authority in respect of the monitoring of the solvency and liquidity of its affiliated credit co-operatives. The savings banks are represented in the Nederlandse Spaarbankbond (Netherlands Savings Bank Association), which has likewise been given supervisory functions. The training of bank staff and research activities are undertaken by the Nederlands Instituut voor het Bank- en Effectenbedrijf (Netherlands Institute for Banking and Securities Business).

4 Belgium

General outline

There are many similarities between the banking system in Belgium and that of the neighbouring Netherlands, with which it co-operates particularly closely within the scope of what is known as the Benelux economic union, together with Luxembourg. Two-thirds of the balance sheet total of all credit institutions are accounted for by depository institutions of the universal type, while public law credit institutions account for just under a quarter and private savings banks for the remaining tenth; the credit co-operative sector plays only a modest role. A number of savings banks have been established in the legal form of credit co-operatives. The Centrale Raiffeisenkas CV (CERA) belongs to the category of universal banks. Most of the banks conducting mainly external business are of foreign origin, or are controlled from abroad. If the structure of the banking system is analysed in terms of outstanding loans to the Belgian private sector, the market share of the depository institutions shrinks to 45%, while that of the private savings banks comes to 41%. The remaining 14% is accounted for by public law credit institutions which lend primarily to the public sector.

Belgium has seen a sharp acceleration of the trend towards despecialisation in the banking sector, although a specific policy of deregulation on the part of the government played an only minor role. What was of far greater significance was the overriding need to deal with fiercer competition. Compared with earlier years, domestic and foreign investors, in particular institutional investors, have developed an increasing awareness of interest rates, and that has caused them to look for alternatives. Their industrial clients have improved their liquidity management, and the general trend towards securitisation in Europe, as well as the influence of Anglo-Saxon investment banking, have resulted in them slightly relaxing their traditional ties to a principal banker. The traditionally leading banks have nevertheless been able even to increase their relatively high market shares to the detriment of the public law specialised institutions.

Role of the Banque Nationale de Belgique

At the top of the banking system in Belgium is the Banque Nationale de Belgique, a type of public limited company, in which the government has a stake of 50%. It has 23 branch offices, some of which are due to be converted into representative offices. As the central bank, it is responsible for issuing banknotes, for managing bank liquidity, and thus for the refinancing of banks. It also acts as the government's banker.

For some years now, the monetary goal of price stability has been pursued via a policy of keeping the value of the Belgian franc stable within the EMS. This is strived for through an adjustment of short term interest rates to those in Germany. In the course of its policy of convergence, the central bank has been increasingly successful in gradually diminishing the interest rate differential, which still had to be kept high in the early 1980s, to the benefit of the Belgian money market rates. At the beginning of 1990, the level of interest rates was determined primarily by a discretionary fixing of the rates for treasury certificates, the issue of which is of key importance to the treasury. The rediscount and Lombard rates had only a marginal impact on the refinancing of banks, and thus on interest rate policy, because the banks were able, at any time, to adjust their portfolios to the treasury certificates.

Monetary policy decisions demanded prior consultations with the Commission Bancaire (Banking Commission) and the approval of the Minister of Finance. Since spring 1990, the set of monetary policy instruments available for a market-conforming management of the money market has gradually been modified so as to make the central bank less dependent on the government. In 1991, the *de facto* linkage to the Bundesbank's interest rate policy was strengthened by the decision to voluntarily reduce the standard margin of exchange rate fluctuation still further within the scope of the EMS intervention mechanism. The central bank's weekly securities repurchase tenders have become the most important monetary policy instrument. The central bank is entitled at any time to intervene through open market operations. The government's access to central bank credit was subject to strict limits even prior to the entry into force of the Maastricht Treaty on 1 January 1994, under which direct central bank lending to the government is forbidden.

As Belgium and Luxembourg have entered into a currency union, decisions on exchange control issues are vested, in principle, in the Institut Belgo–Luxembourgeois du Change (Belgian–Luxembourg Foreign Exchange Institute), while the Banque Nationale de Belgique deals with their technical implementation. At the beginning of 1990, however, the abolition of the system of dual exchange rates for the free exchange market (involving primarily capital transactions) on the one hand, and for the regulated market on the other, saw the revocation of the last capital controls in both Belgium and Luxembourg.

Institut de Réescompte et de Garantie

A Royal Decree led to the establishment, in 1935, of the Institut de Réescompte et de Garantie (IRG; Institute for Rediscounting and Guarantees) to assist banks and other enterprises in mobilising their claims or to support them with special loans in emergencies. The capital of the IRG is held by 39 banks and 5 private savings banks. Up until the money market reforms at the beginning of 1991, the Institute played a key role as a market maker on the money market. Subject to terms and conditions determined by the Banque Nationale de Belgique, the IRG rediscounted short term bills of exchange in favour of banks and placed short to medium term bills in the market. On the basis of an agreement reached between the group of the banks and that of the private savings banks, the IRG was commissioned in 1985 to manage two deposit guarantee funds for these institutions.

Legislation and banking supervision

1935 saw the establishment for banking supervision purposes of the legally independent Commission Bancaire (Banking Commission), which is also responsible for supervising security issues, investment funds and *sociétés à portefeuille* (securities companies providing venture capital). Since 1993, it has been known as the Commission Bancaire et Financière (Banking and Finance Commission). Since reforms in 1975 and 1980, banking supervision has covered all banks which regularly accept deposits with maturities of up to two years and use these funds for lending or investment, as well as the private savings banks. Under the provisions of the Act of 10 June 1964, it also applied to the relatively insignificant category of financing institutions and – on behalf of the Minister of Finance – to the Caisse Générale d'Epargne et de Retraite (General Savings and Pensions Bank) within the category of public law credit institutions.

Another major and radical step was marked by legislation passed on 22 March 1993, which applied to all categories of credit institutions, subjecting them all to the same rules regarding their status and supervision. That legislation also translated both the EC Directive of December 1989 on banking co-ordination and the EC Directive of April 1991 concerning the supervision of credit institutions on a consolidated basis into Belgian national law. In line with the principle of a reciprocal recognition of the status and licences granted in another EU member state, responsibility for the supervision of branches established in Belgium of credit institutions from other EU countries, as well as of the services they render, is now vested in the appropriate authorities of the country of origin. In addition, the law permits credit institutions to acquire, among other things, participating interests in industrial and commercial enterprises.

Market shares and international links of the individual categories of banks

On 24 January 1989, there were 86 banks in all, with more than 3600 branches and a balance sheet total of BFr 10 971 billion (at the end of 1988), which came to two-thirds of the balance sheet total of all the credit institutions subject to banking supervision. Only 29 of these institutions were of predominantly Belgian origin; 33 foreign institutions had branches in Belgium and a further 24 institutions established under Belgian law were controlled from abroad. Roughly half of the foreign banks were from other EU countries (including 13 French banks), while the other half came from outside the EU (including 15 from Japan). Half the balance sheet total was accounted for by foreign banks or banks controlled from abroad. Although the share of foreign banks in business with domestic clients, including interbank business, was somewhat smaller, they nevertheless accounted for 34% of total assets and 26% of liabilities. However, foreign banks dominate cross-border credit relations, with a share of 62%.

Viewed in analytical terms, most of the foreign, or foreign-controlled, banks belong to the category of money market banks. A second category comprises small to medium-sized banks, which hold a significant proportion of the deposits of households and small businesses, and which use these funds for investment in public bonds and in the interbank market. The third category of 'diversified' banks encompasses only a small number of institutions, which are of outstanding significance in terms of their size, however. They have a close-knit network of banking outlets.

Universal banks

The three largest banks are the Générale de Banque SA, the Banque Bruxelles Lambert SA and the Kredietbank NV. The already relatively high degree of concentration has tended to increase even further in the last few years. At the end of 1988, 70% of all loans to households and corporate clients were accounted for by the five largest banks. In the field of non-bank deposits, their market share came to as much as 79%. The legal distinction between depository institutions and holding companies, which came into effect in 1935, has largely been reversed as a result of the many exceptions that have had to be made. Even before the new banking law of March 1993 entered into force, it had been possible for them to acquire stock of, or participating interests in, credit institutions. Purchases of participatory securities had also been permitted generally if it was intended to sell them within, at most, three years, or if such securities were purchased in exchange for bad loans, for a maximum of two years, an initial period which could be extended by the Commission Bancaire.

Public law specialised credit institutions

The general trend towards a diversification of business activities has recently been particularly marked in the case of public law specialised credit institutions. In 1989, this category encompassed three very large institutions for long term savings, for industrial credit and for local authority loans, and also included a number of smaller institutions. The largest specialised institution, which has a share of some 9% in the overall credit market, is the Crédit Communal de Belgique (CCB). It provides the provincial and local governments with predominantly long term, both securitised and unsecuritised credit. Recently, in the wake of the 1991 Act to restructure the Belgian public banking sector, it has added industrial and mortgage lending to its range of business through mergers with two other public law banks. It refinances itself primarily through the issue of medium and long term bonds, but increasingly also accepts sight, time and savings deposits from individuals and public authorities. The institution's shareholders are the provincial and local governments in Belgium.

Of almost equal size is the Caisse Générale d'Epargne et de Retraite (CGER), likewise one of the largest credit institutions in Belgium and one of the largest savings banks in the world. The institution, which dates back to 1865, obtains most of its refinancing through savings deposits and savings bonds, and provides loans to the public sector, for housing construction purposes and, to a minor extent, to finance industry and exports. To this is added the life and property insurance business conducted via a subsidiary. Only recently, after mergers with public sector industrial and mortgage lending institutions, its name has been changed to ASLK-CGER. In September 1993, the Belgian–Dutch insurance group Fortis acquired a stake of 49.9% in it as part of the government's privatisation programme.

The balance sheet total of the Société Nationale de Crédit à l'Industrie (SNCI), which specialises in medium and long term loans to industrial, agricultural and distribution companies and which covers almost 90% of its refinancing needs on the capital market, was less than half that of the CGER. The government holds 50% of the SNCI's capital, and also guarantees 50% of its lending.

Savings banks

The private savings banks have advanced very far along the road towards becoming universal banks, even though they are still subject to certain investment provisions that favour lending to the public sector and also, albeit to a lesser degree, mortgage loans. On 24 January 1989, there were 31 savings banks, of which 23 were established in the legal form of public limited companies and 7 as co-operative savings institutions, while one was a branch of the BHW Bausparkasse GmbH in Hameln, concentrating on typical building and loan association business with members of staff of the EU institutions. The savings banks, as well as ASLK-CGER, are shareholders of an investment company which may, in turn, acquire participating interests of up to 49% in newly established enterprises. The two largest private savings banks, both of which are established in the form of credit co-operatives, are CERA and Bacob

Savings Bank. Traditionally, the former is the bank of the co-operative agricultural sector, while the latter has its roots in the Christian Workers' Movement. Both of these banks are active mainly in Flanders, where the mutualist movement took hold more strongly, for historical and cultural reasons specific to that region.

Associations of the banking sector and their members

Belgium's banks are members of the Association Belge des Banques (Belgian Banking Association), which represents their interests. The private savings banks are members of the Association des Caisses d'Epargne Privées (Association of Private Savings Banks), while the public law specialised credit institutions represent their own interests or have them represented by the Minister of Finance. Statutory provisions stipulate that the banking associations must be consulted before the relevant public bodies take decisions on a number of monetary policy and banking supervision issues, and consultations are the rule in other areas as well.

Most of the EU central banking associations (see Appendix 3) also have offices in Brussels. They now play a key advisory role in the process of harmonising national banking supervision regulations at a European level.

5 *Luxembourg*

General outline

Luxembourg is by far the smallest member state of the EU, with a total population of only 365 000. An economic and monetary union, which dates back to 1922, links the country particularly closely to Belgium, the larger partner in that union. Since the mid-1960s, however, Luxembourg has systematically developed its local financial market, which has an insignificant economic hinterland of its own, into one of the world's leading financial centres. Its ascent is closely associated with the expansion of the Euro-money and Euro-capital markets. It competes fiercely with London and other, well-established financial centres in Europe, the relative importance of which has recently risen in the wake of the elimination of capital controls and the envisaged harmonisation of competitive conditions in the EU.

Role of the Institut Monétaire Luxembourgeois

The country does not have a central bank in the normal sense of the word. The Institut Monétaire Luxembourgeois

(IML), which was established in 1983, is responsible not only for the supervision of both banking and securities transactions but also for the development of Luxembourg as a financial centre generally and, within strict limits, for the issue of banknotes. Together with the Banking Association, it could well determine the terms and conditions governing bank credit. In practice, however, the currency union with Belgium has left the IML with no scope for the pursuit of exchange and interest rate policies of its own, and prevents it, in particular, from functioning independently as a lender of last resort. It is the public Caisse d'Epargne de l'Etat (CEE), which was established as early as 1856, that functions as both the government's banker and the credit institutions' clearing centre. As the CEE carries by far the major proportion of domestic savings, which it uses predominantly to grant medium to long term loans to public and private borrowers in Luxembourg, the Minister of Finance is able – to a limited extent – to directly influence conditions on the local financial markets.

Banking supervision

As the competent banking supervisory authority, the IML is responsible for supervising all credit institutions in the Grand Duchy of Luxembourg that accept, on a commercial basis, deposits or other repayable funds with the intention of lending or investing them for their own accounts. Included are all banks, savings institutions and credit cooperatives, to the extent that they accept sight and short term savings or time deposits, as well as non-bank financial institutions, which are entitled to accept funds with maturities of less than two years solely from the aforementioned credit institutions. The IML is also responsible for the supervision of investment funds. 1992 and 1993 saw the adoption and entry into force of a number of banking laws and regulations which translated EC Directives into Luxembourg national law.

Market shares of the categories of banks

The number of banks and savings institutions increased further to 169 in 1988 and 1989. At the end of 1989, their consolidated balance sheet total came to LFr 11 337 billion. In addition, there were 48 agricultural credit co-operatives and 21 other financial institutions, which had a combined share of only 0.6% in the business of all credit institutions and which are not included in officially published figures. The number of people employed in the banking sector totalled 15 000, which represented 8.4% of the total number of employed in Luxembourg. 44% of that total were non-residents.

In 1989 alone, the number of *organismes de placement collectif* (OPC; investment funds), which are not deemed to be credit institutions in the legal sense, rose by 126 to 651. The assets managed by these funds expanded by no less than 39%, to a total of LFr 2964 billion.

Domestic universal banks

In addition to the public savings bank CEE, there are three other important domestic banks which have extensive branch networks and are also represented abroad, namely the Banque Générale du Luxembourg (BGL), the Banque Internationale à Luxembourg (BIL) and the Kredietbank SA Luxembourgeoise (KBL). They are affiliated to the three large Belgian financial groups, but operate relatively independently. In the field of savings business, they compete with both the CEE and the Postal Savings Bank. The large domestic banks also conduct international lending and deposit business on a considerable scale. This holds true, above all, of deposits of funds (denominated in Belgian francs) from Belgium.

Domestic specialised banks

The category of domestic specialised banks encompasses, most importantly, the Caisse Hypothécaire du Luxembourg SA, the Société Nationale de Crédit et d'Investissement (SNCI), and the rural credit co-operatives under the lead of the Caisse Centrale Raiffeisen. The SNCI was established in 1977 to provide small and medium-sized businesses with medium to long term investment loans and export credit, as well as guarantees and participating interests, and it receives funds for that purpose from the government or raises the funds needed on the domestic capital market.

Presence of foreign and foreign-controlled banks in Luxembourg

At the end of 1989, only 19 of the total of 166 banks and savings institutions established in Luxembourg either as public limited companies under Luxembourg law (140) or as branches of foreign banks (26), came from Luxembourg or Belgium. The leading position was held by German banks, 33 of which had set up offices in Luxembourg; generally these took the form of independent subsidiaries, but in some cases branches, and occasionally both. Switzerland and France were represented by 14 banks each, the United States by 11 banks, Italy and Japan by 9 banks each, the Netherlands by 5 banks, and the Scandinavian banks (as a group) by 21 institutions. To the extent that their activities are reflected in the balance sheet statistics, they conduct almost exclusively Euro-lending, Euro-money market and Euro-deposit business.

Interestingly, some 85% of all assets and liabilities are denominated in foreign currency rather than in Luxembourg's domestic currency; the bulk of this is accounted for by cross-border operations.

Appendix: Luxembourg and the Euro-market

In view of the outstanding weight of Euro-banking transactions in overall banking business in Luxembourg, it seems appropriate to analyse that part separately and to compare it with the Euro-business in other European banking centres (see Table 3).

The analysis is therefore based on the figures of the balance sheet statistics of the Bank for International Settlements in Basle for a total of 15 European reporting countries. Excluded therefore are the European or foreign currency transactions of banks in North America, in Japan and in the six major offshore financial centres in Asia and the Caribbean and – on grounds relating to the comparability of the figures – the foreign currency transactions with resident banks and non-banks in the 15 European reporting countries (business that plays a relatively prominent role in both London and Tokyo, the two leading Euro-market centres).

Market shares, broken down by Euro-market centre

By the end of 1989, the market share of banks in Luxembourg had risen to about 11.5% (US $1956 billion) in external Euro-assets, and to 9.6% ($2147 billion) in external Euro-liabilities. Luxembourg thus ranked third behind London and Paris on the liabilities side, but ahead of Brussels, Amsterdam and Frankfurt, the leading financial centres in the respective reporting countries. Lending business there is concentrated more markedly than in other European countries on transactions involving banks and non-banks in Western Europe, which account for 70% of such operations, as against an average share of 46% for all banks in Europe. The remainder is accounted for by other countries in Eastern Europe and on other continents.

The proportion of loans granted direct to non-bank clients has always been particularly high in Luxembourg, although it declined from 54% in 1983 to 37% at the end of 1989. A special type of credit that has come to prominence, in addition to short term trade credit, is that of medium to long term, syndicated, 'roll-over' Euro-credit, where the interest rate is fixed in the form of a predetermined spread *vis-à-vis* the interbank rate in Luxembourg or London (with the latter being referred to as 'LIBOR', or the London Interbank Offered Rate). The actual interest rate is thus adjusted to the current trend in the Euro-money market rates of the agreed Euro-currency on the roll-over date every three or six months. This keeps the lending bank's interest rate risk within very strict limits.

Market shares, broken down by Euro-currency

Although the Euro-loans granted to public or private bodies may be true financial credits or balance of payments credits, the Euro-banks prefer direct loans to finance exports or certain investments, for instance. The leading currency used for Euro-lending in Luxembourg is the Deutsche Mark, which has a share of 38%, while that of the Euro-dollar comes to only 32% (for the market shares in respect of Euro-liabilities, see Table 3). Use of the Swiss franc for lending is tending to decline as well, while the share of the ECU has risen to as much as 4.4%.

Where Euro-banking in Europe as a whole is concerned, shaped as it is predominantly by Euro-operations in London and Paris, the Euro-dollar has traditionally been the leading lending currency, although its share has

Table 3 *Euro-deposits of banks in Luxembourg and other European financial centres*

End of the period	**1986**	**1987**	**1988**	**1989**
Banks in Europe[1]				
Euro-liabilities				
Total in US$ billion	1504.5	1867.5	1916.0	2147.1
Annual growth in %	+23.4	+24.1	+2.6	+12.1
Broken down by currency (in %)				
US dollar	60.3	54.5	54.6	51.8
Deutsche Mark	14.9	16.8	16.4	18.6
Yen	5.6	7.3	6.5	7.1
Swiss franc	6.9	7.3	5.7	5.4
ECU	3.2	3.5	3.9	4.3
Others	9.1	10.6	12.9	12.8
Broken down by sector (in %)				
Banking sector	81.7	81.9	81.3	80.9
Non-banking sector	18.3	18.1	18.7	19.1
Broken down by financial centre (in %)				
United Kingdom	46.4	44.6	44.1	42.4
France	13.3	13.4	13.9	14.6

Luxembourg	8.5	8.9	8.8	9.6
Belgium	8.3	8.6	8.0	7.8
Netherlands	4.5	4.7	5.0	4.9
Italy	4.7	4.6	4.8	4.3
Others	14.3	15.2	15.4	16.6
Banks in Luxembourg				
Euro-liabilities				
Total in US$ billion	128.7	166.1	168.6	206.7
Annual growth in %	+31.1	+29.5	+1.5	+22.6
Broken down by currency (in %)				
US dollar	36.6	32.1	32.9	27.0
Deutsche Mark	39.6	40.7	38.5	41.5
Yen	1.2	1.3	1.4	1.5
Swiss franc	9.2	10.5	8.7	8.5
ECU	3.6	3.8	3.4	3.7
Others	9.8	11.6	15.1	17.8
Broken down by sector (in %)				
Banking sector	78.3	75.6	70.7	63.8
Non-banking sector	21.7	24.4	29.3	36.2

Sources: Bank for International Settlements (BIS) and Institut Monétaire Luxembourgeois (IML).

1 Ten EU member states (excluding Greece and Portugal) and five non-EU countries (Austria, Finland, Norway, Sweden and Switzerland).

dropped from just under 75% at the beginning of the 1980s to 53% at the end of 1989. Next in importance are the Deutsche Mark (16%), the Japanese yen (9%) and the Swiss franc as well as the ECU (both 5%). In the last few years, progressive liberalisation has seen a significant increase in the market shares of other Euro-currencies, such as the pound sterling, the French franc and the Italian lira. This did not, however, prevent the Deutsche Mark from perceptibly increasing its lead over other EU currencies in cross-border Euro-business in the 1980s. Another remarkable development is the fact that the ECU – which although a 'near-Deutsche Mark' currency unit on account of the weight (almost one-third) given to the German currency in the basket, reflects the weighted trend in the value of all EU currencies so that it might serve as an alternative to leading Euro-currencies – now ranks second in intra-EU business.

In principle, this also holds true of the liabilities side of the Euro-market, although it must be mentioned that the growth of the ECU market in the 1980s was more pronounced on the lending side than on the deposit side (refinancing by Euro-banks; see Table 3).

The particularly sharp increase in the share of the Euro-Deutsche Mark in the last few years was due to the fact that banks, industrial enterprises and individuals in Germany invested a considerable proportion of the high German current account surpluses in the Euro-Deutsche Mark market, primarily with banks in London, Luxembourg and Paris. However, the minimum amounts needed for such Euro-time deposits are relatively high. One of the reasons why Euro-deposits are attractive to non-banks is that they are not subject to minimum reserve requirements. For a number of years now, the Euro-banks have passed on the arithmetic advantage such deposits have over Deutsche Mark deposits in Germany (where non-interest-bearing minimum reserves must be held at the Deutsche Bundesbank) preferably to depositors (via comparatively higher interest rates on credit balances) than to borrowers. The minimum reserve ratios on sight deposits with maturities of less than 30 days and on time deposits were 12.1% and 4.95%, respectively, but have since been cut to 5% (from 1 March 1994) and 2% (from 1 March 1993), respectively.

Increasing use of non-bank Euro-deposits for refinancing purposes

All of the above has contributed significantly to a radical change in the way Euro-business is refinanced in Luxembourg. Whereas Euro-banks in Luxembourg were formerly renowned predominantly for granting cross-border Euro-loans to non-banks (primarily to clients in Germany), which they refinanced almost exclusively on the international interbank market, the proportion of their refinancing obtained through non-bank deposits surged upwards from 22% in 1986 to 36% in 1989.

This went hand in hand with an expansion of their business with individual clients, which is far more labour-intensive than that with corporate and public clients. Increasing competition with London, Paris and Brussels in traditional Euro-business has also led to their endeavouring intensively to secure typical investment banking business. However, these endeavours come up against strict limits not only in terms of the competitive strength of London and other European financial centres, but also on account of the banking strategies pursued by the management of the individual groups to gain an optimum position in the single European market for financial services.

6 United Kingdom

General outline

The British banking system differs from the systems of continental Europe in several respects. It was long regarded as an exemplary model of a clear division of labour, even though that division was due not to statutory provisions, as is the case in the United States and Japan, but rather to historic demarcations which developed over time and were largely self-imposed. Clear functional distinctions were made between major business areas, namely between commercial banking, investment banking, housing finance, insurance business portfolio management and securities trading. In the 1970s and 1980s, the British banking system, too, was affected by the trend towards institutional diversification that automatically resulted from the liberalisation and deregulation of the financial system. The development of new technologies and the ever-heavier pressure of competition fostered the introduction of a great number of innovative financial instruments and markets. However, banking business was never separated from deposit business or refinancing through borrowing; in order to be recognised as a bank, an institution must not only deal exclusively in lending, but must, among other things, take deposits.

The Banking Act of 1979 still distinguished between 'recognised banks' and 'licensed deposit-taking institutions'. However, that distinction was abolished with the Banking Act of 1987, which introduced the uniform term of 'authorised institution'. Any authorised institution with equity capital and general reserves totalling at least £5 million has the right to call itself a bank. Although the major clearing banks conduct securities operations – both for their own accounts and for the accounts of third parties – on a considerable scale, either directly or via subsidiary securities trading firms, portfolio transactions do not require a banking licence as such, but are subject to separate supervision governed by the Financial Services Act of 1986.

Another feature of the British financial system is the relatively great significance of well-organised short and long term financial markets, on which securitised financial claims or standardised options and financial futures contracts on such claims are traded. The major structural changes recorded in the last few years, most of which are associated with the 'Big Bang' on the London Stock Exchange of October 1986, have virtually done away with the strict principle of specialisation. Yet, while this has led to the increased participation of financially strong domestic banks as well as foreign banks and securities houses in securities business, both as brokers and as market makers, this has by no means diminished the role played by these markets.

The British banking system is marked by a high concentration of banks in the City of London, where about one-fifth of all bank employees in the United Kingdom work. The City of London attained its outstanding position in the nineteenth and early twentieth centuries when the pound sterling was the world's leading reserve currency. After the Second World

War, London developed into the leading offshore financial centre for Euro-transactions. The Euro-dollar and other foreign currencies had largely replaced the pound sterling as an international lending and investment currency, but in the 1980s, after all remaining international exchange rate restrictions had been lifted in 1979, the British currency achieved something of a comeback.

Structure and functions of the Bank of England

The Bank of England is the United Kingdom's central bank. It was established as a private institution in 1694, and nationalised in 1946. As a public entity, it has the right to manage its own internal affairs. However, Article 4 of the Bank of England Act of 1946 stipulates that 'the Treasury may from time to time give such directions to the Bank as, after consultation with the Governor of the Bank, they think necessary in the public interest'. Although the Treasury has never to date issued any formal directions, what is decisive in cases of conflict in interest and exchange rate policy is that it has the potential to do so. The Bank of England's supreme decision-making body is the Court of Directors, which consists of the Governor, the Deputy Governor and four executive directors as well as twelve part-time directors, who are appointed by the Crown, i.e. by the Prime Minister, upon proposal by the Chancellor of the Exchequer. The banknotes issued by the Bank of England are entered into the Issue Department's balance sheet on the liabilities side, a balance sheet which is kept separate from that of the Banking Department. They are covered on the assets side by, among other things, commercial bills, promissory notes, government securities, balances held with the Banking Department and 'other' assets.

In addition to its responsibility for issuing banknotes, the Bank of England has key functions in the field of payments and clearing, acts as the banking system's lender of last resort, is responsible for banking supervision, functions as the government's banker and is responsible, in particular, for the implementation of monetary, reserve and exchange rate policies. The Chancellor of the Exchequer decides on any changes in interest rates, and makes the appropriate announcements. Since early 1994, however, the advice the Bank of England gives the government on the proper level of interest rates has been published in the minutes of the monthly meetings of the Governor and the Chancellor of the Exchequer, with only a short delay so as to strengthen the position of the Bank of England. This also makes both the setting of the monetary policy objectives, the final goal of which is the achievement of monetary (domestic price) stability, and the determination of the monetary policy stance, as open and transparent a process as possible. The Bank of England also publishes a quarterly report on inflation.

In the 1980s, the Bank of England's use of interest rate policy was not geared unilaterally to controlling the money stock M3 or certain other monetary aggregates, or even the monetary base M0. The trends in both monetary reserves and the exchange rates, as well as the net public sector borrowing requirements, have likewise been key indicators for its monetary policy, at least temporarily. The most important instruments used by the Bank of England to implement its interest rate targets were open market operations on the rediscount market to influence the level of short-term interest rates and interventions in the market for treasury bonds. From time to time, foreign exchange intervention has played a supporting role as well; it did so initially in the late 1980s when the pound shadowed the Deutsche Mark, and then predominantly in the period from October 1990 to September 1992 when the United Kingdom was a participant in the exchange rate mechanism of the EMS (although on the basis of a wider fluctuation margin of ±6% *vis-à-vis* the officially-fixed bilateral central rates).

Following the pound sterling's withdrawal from the exchange rate mechanism, together with the Italian lira, the new underlying monetary policy stance has been to use interest rate measures to keep inflation in the range of between 1% and 4%, with the intention, in the longer term, of bringing it down to below 2½%. The Bank of England remains ready from day to day to undertake open market operations so as to ensure that money market rates in the decisive one-month to three-month maturity range do not diverge too markedly or for too long a period from the official dealing rates. This need to intervene on a daily basis is a consequence of the Bank of England's regime of reserve requirements, namely a zero reserve requirement with a maintenance period of only one day (the cash deposit ratio of 0.35% at the time of writing, is in place purely for purposes of generating income). This stands in contrast to the Bundesbank's practice, for instance, of continuing to rely essentially on a liquidity buffer for banks (albeit a reduced one), which is created by requiring specific non-interest-bearing minimum reserves to be maintained with the Bundesbank on an average each calendar month.

Since January 1994, the Bank of England's day-to-day operations in the eligible bills' market have been supplemented by new repo and secured loan facilities, which have become a permanent feature of its money market operations. Funds are provided through repos involving gilt-edged stock and loans secured by certain government-guaranteed securities which are in more ample supply than commercial bills. The rate of interest on such funds, which are made available for fixed periods of two or four weeks every fortnight, is fixed in advance and closely related to the rate at which the Bank of England provides funds through its daily bill operations. The volume is determined after the applications have come in. While bill operations continue to be effected with discount houses as the privileged counterparties for channelling liquidity from the central bank to the banking system, a key feature of the new facilities is also that the counterparties include large banks and building societies as well as market-makers in gilt-edged securities.

Retail banks

Domestic banking business is dominated by 21 depository institutions which handle the deposit and credit operations of the retail (personal) sector (clearing and other retail banks; see Table 4). At the end of 1989, they accounted for about a quarter of the business volume of all banks and building societies, and for as much as a third of all sterling business. Their most important competitors are the building societies. Six of the depository institutions have nationwide networks of branch offices, namely the four largest clearing banks – National Westminster, Lloyds, Barclays and Midland – as well as the TSB Bank Group (a merger of the formerly independent Trustee Savings Banks), and the Girobank. The Midland has recently become a member of the Hong Kong and Shanghai Banking Group. The other depository institutions are regional in character. In mid-1989, the Abbey National plc, which had previously been operated as a building society, was recognised as a bank.

Irrespective of the leading role they play in the field of bulk business, the depository institutions also cover the whole range of corporate and international banking services, either directly or via subsidiary institutions. The share of their total sterling liabilities accounted for by the deposits of major clients had risen to more than 63% as early as 1985. Where their sterling assets are concerned, three-fifths of their short term working fund lending takes the form of overdraft loans.

Interest rates are determined largely by market forces. This also holds true of basic lending rates which, although fixed by the individual banks involved, are closely aligned

Table 4 *Structure of the British banking system*[1] *(at the end of 1989)*

	Balance sheet total		Deposits in £ billion	
	in £ billion	**in %**	**Sterling**	**Other currencies**
Banks in the United Kingdom[2]	1237.1	86.0	471.2	667.9
Clearing and other retail banks	391.5	27.2	266.4	63.5
British merchant banks	51.4	3.6	28.9	15.8
Other British banks[2]	64.4	4.5	40.2	12.4
Foreign banks	729.8	50.7	135.5	576.1
of which: Banks from the United States	118.7	8.2	17.3	96.8
Banks from Japan	282.0	19.6	33.3	246.3
Discount houses	15.3	1.0	14.5	0.4
Building societies[3]	188.7	13.1	168.5	2.0
Total (unconsolidated)	**1441.1**	**100**	**654.2**	**670.3**

Source: Bank of England, Quarterly Bulletin; Financial Statistics, *London, HMSO.*

1 Excluding finance companies, National Savings Bank, specialised financial institutions.

2 Including banks submitting quarterly reports.

3 Excluding Abbey National Building Society; since July 1989, the institutions of the Abbey National Group have been classified as banks.

to the marginal refinancing costs on the interbank market. The total interest due on fixed-term loans to the corporate sector is based directly on the relevant interbank rate. Whenever current accounts are carried on the basis of appropriate credit balances, there are no charges on normal payment services.

The key role played by depository institutions in bulk business can be seen from the fact that they maintained a total of some 13 700 branch offices of all kinds at the end of 1989. The bank with the largest number of branches at the end of 1988 was National Westminster (3086), followed by Barclays (2712), Lloyds (2189), Midland (2090), TSB (1546), The Royal Bank of Scotland (829) and, finally, the Bank of Scotland (540). Roughly 70% of all adults in the United Kingdom have a current account, and more than a third have a deposit account.

There are three independent clearing organisations under the umbrella of the Association for Payment Clearing Services. One undertakes the clearing of cheques and credit transfers. Another is responsible for the same-day clearing of large-value payments, either electronically for the whole country (CHAPS = Clearing House Automated Payment System), or paper-based for the City of London (Town Clearing). The third system is also electronic and clears the bulk of standing orders and direct debits (Bankers Automated Clearing Services). Membership is open to any bank or other financial institution that has a share of at least 0.5% in the total clearing volume.

All major retail banks maintain large networks of multipurpose banking machines which provide clients with 24-hour access to cash and a number of other banking services. There were some 11 300 banking machines in operation at the end of 1989. The banks provide their clients not only with cheque guarantee cards of their own but also with standardised Euro-cheque forms and Euro-cheque cards. Credit cards are a popular means of payment. At the end of 1988, 32 financial institutions had issued Visa credit cards, e.g. Barclaycard, to 17 million clients. The number of Access cards, credit cards integrated into the MasterCard system, totalled 13 million. Some 43% of all adults in the United Kingdom had at least one credit card at the end of 1988. Many depository institutions, as well as building societies, offer their clients terminals which allow them to effect banking transactions from their homes. In addition, there are now quite a number of point-of-sale systems, with a total of 30 000 terminals in retail shops and travel bureaus, which provide for an immediate electronic debiting of a customer's bank account.

Wholesale banks

By tradition, all banks that are not deemed to be retail banks are classified as wholesale banks. At the beginning of 1990, this category encompassed 31 British merchant banks, 170 other British banks, more than 360 foreign banks and, finally, 8 discount houses which form a category of highly specialised banks. Most of the wholesale banks are commercial banks geared to business with corporate clients. The category is far more heterogeneous than that of the large retail banks, and is marked by a number of peculiarities.

As can be seen from Table 4, foreign currency Euro-transactions are of far greater significance than sterling transactions. The foreign banks, which understandably enough, account for a major proportion of Euro-currency business, are nevertheless endeavouring to gain ground in domestic sterling operations. Two-fifths of sterling deposits are time rather than sight deposits. Sight deposits, in turn, are generally not demand deposits, which can be disposed of by cheques, but rather interest-bearing day-to-day money.

As in the case of Euro-currency transactions, the banks demand minimum deposits of £10 000 or more for time deposits, so that small private clients are virtually excluded. Many sterling deposits are taken in via the sterling interbank market. More than two-fifths of the assets are money market loans and stocks of certificates of deposit. Almost half the balance sheet total is usually accounted for by loans granted to large corporate customers in the form of fixed-term loans, instead of – as is the case with the large retail banks – in the form of current account credit.

Merchant banks

Many merchant banks were formerly simple trading companies with worldwide connections that used trade bills as their main means of effecting payments. In line with the increase in both their standing and financial power, they realised that the acceptance of trade bills issued by less renowned traders could become a profitable business. Above all, trading companies established in London seized the opportunities offered when the pound sterling became an international currency and was generally accepted in payment.

Although international short and medium term lending continues to play a dominant role today, portfolio management services for institutional investors (which are usually provided via specialised subsidiaries), the provision of capital market advice and finance, the financing of corporate take-overs and the provision or arrangement of venture capital are of significance as well. In addition, most merchant banks operate in other sectors, e.g. in the marketing of insurance products, in shipping, in the gold trade and in the real estate sector. Many merchant banks have become very active in the securities business, not least by taking over stockbrokers and traders in the wake of the stock exchange reforms effected since the mid-1980s. A number of merchant banks have developed into international financial conglomerates which compete fiercely with major domestic and international securities companies, while others have remained relatively small and specialise in profitable market niches.

Other British banks

Numerically the largest category is that of 'other' British banks. Very heterogeneous in structure, many are subsidiaries of major retail banks, or are of only local or regional significance. Some major banks have their headquarters in London, but maintain extensive branch networks in certain regions abroad, above all in Latin America and eastern Asia, as well as, to a lesser extent, in Africa. The largest bank in this field is the Standard Chartered Bank, which has a number of subsidiaries and participating interests abroad; in continental Europe, it co-operates with, among others, West LB (Chartered West LB Ltd). Grindlays Bank has an extensive network of branches in Africa, Asia and the Near East, but was taken over by ANZ Bank in 1984 and so has become a foreign bank, though nevertheless still retains its head office in London.

Foreign banks

Measured in terms of the balance sheet total, roughly half of all banking business, including that of the building societies, is accounted for by foreign banks (see Table 4). At the end of February 1990, there were 346 foreign banks, including branches and minority holdings in banking consortiums operating in the United Kingdom, largely based in London. 45 of these came from the United States, and 32 from Japan. The share of the Japanese banks in the balance sheet total of all foreign banks came to about two-fifths. They likewise accounted for two-fifths of all foreign currency business in the United Kingdom, so that their business share in both cases was several times larger than that of either the US or the British banks. Another 184 foreign banks had representative offices. The total number of people employed by foreign banks exceeded 70 000 at the end of 1987.

In this context, it must also be taken into consideration that more than 120 foreign securities houses, most of which come from Japan, the United States and Canada, have offices in London. They are not banks in the formal definition, i.e. they do not have a banking licence, and are subject to the formal supervision of the Securities and Investment Board (SIB) or The Securities Association (TSA) which is a self-ruling body. All major names are represented in the TSA. They have contributed decisively to the fact that London is the main centre of not only the Euro-lending and Euro-money markets but also the Eurobond market. Citibank from the United States is the only foreign bank that is striving purposely and successfully to penetrate the domestic market for personal loan and deposit business. It is also an acknowledged clearing bank in CHAPS and Town Clearing.

Discount houses

The ten discount houses (until recently there were only eight) fulfil a special function in the British financial system. They act as special intermediaries between the Bank of England and the banking sector, handle the offsetting of short term funds between the government and the banks, and have committed themselves bindingly to guarantee the placement of the weekly issues, under a tender procedure, of three-month treasury bills. Conversely, the discount houses enjoy traditionally privileged access to the Bank of England as a lender of last resort in day-to-day money market management. Where the fortnightly repos (introduced in early 1990) are concerned, however, they are required – as mentioned earlier – to share that access with the large retail banks and building societies as well as with market-makers in gilt-edged securities. The discount houses' assets are primarily treasury and trade bills, current short-term government bonds and local authority securities as well as fungible certificates of deposit denominated in both sterling and US dollars.

Building societies

Insofar as they have not applied for or received banking licences, building societies are not deemed to be banks. They are mutual associations owned by their own savers and borrowers. Their business is supervised by the Building Societies Commission. In contrast to the situation in German building and loan associations, savers are entitled to withdraw their deposits immediately or after a short period of notice. By tradition, the building societies grant variable interest rate, long term loans to finance housing. More than 70% of adults in the United Kingdom have an account at a building society. Although the major retail banks have been granting an increasing volume of housing loans for some time now, particularly since 1985, the building societies are still the most important lenders in this field.

The Building Societies Act of 1986 has led to an intensification of competition between banks and building societies. To an increasing extent building societies, which often have a close-knit network of branches, also offer cheque accounts, cash facilities, unsecured loans, not to mention credit card and investment services. Since 1988, building societies have been permitted to raise up to 40% of the funds they require on the market outside the group of their own savers. Since January 1990, they have been able to use 17.5% of their assets for purposes other than that of senior mortgage loans on owner-occupied housing.

This will cause the differences between banks and building societies to diminish further in future. The opportunity to change the legal form of establishment and formally apply for a banking licence was taken successfully in 1989 by Abbey National plc. At the end of 1988, there were 131 registered mutual associations, 110 of which (not counting Abbey National) were members of the Building Societies Association. The three largest institutions – Halifax, Nationwide Anglia and Woolwich – accounted for almost half the total assets.

Other financial institutions

A bank of major significance not included in the group covered by the Bank of England is the National Savings Bank, based in Glasgow. It carries 20 million accounts, with the funds involved being disposable either by post or via the network of 20 000 post offices. It offers ordinary accounts, higher-interest investment accounts with taxable interest payments, tax-free savings certificates at fixed interest or low-indexed interest rates as well as premium bonds, in respect of which the interest is allotted in the form of prizes. At the end of February 1991, it had received funds totalling £36.5 billion which were generally invested in government securities.

The financial institutions outside the banking sector also include investment institutions, such as life insurance companies, pension funds and investment funds. There are also a number of specialised institutions, called finance houses, such as instalment credit institutions, leasing and factoring firms as well as institutions providing venture capital. The larger finance houses are members of the Finance Houses Association (FHA), most members of which have been granted the status of 'authorised institutions' under the provisions of the Banking Act of 1987. Many of these finance houses are owned by banks.

Associations of the banking sector and their members

In the United Kingdom, primarily in the City of London, there are a great number of banking associations and other organisations that represent private financial institutions. They play a major role within the scope of self-rule and the recognition of market rules, although ultimate responsibility for banking supervision is vested in the Bank of England, while the Securities and Investment Board is responsible for supervising securities transactions and other financial services.

The most important association is The British Bankers' Association (BBA) which has its offices at 10 Lombard Street, London EC3V 9EL. The BBA keeps out of the public eye and deals with issues relating to taxation, to legal provisions and to supervisory law. To that extent, it is a major link between government institutions and the banking sector. It is an umbrella association for a number of group associations, such as The Committee of London and Scottish Bankers (CLSB), which is dominated by clearing banks in England and Scotland. There is also The Committee of Scottish Clearing Bankers. A key role in the officially recognised training of banking experts is played by The Chartered Institute of Bankers; in addition, there is the Institute of Bankers in Scotland, based in Edinburgh.

1988 saw the establishment of the British Merchant Banking and Securities Houses Association (BMBA), a merger of the Accepting Houses Committee (AHC) and the Issuing Houses Association (IHA), which dated back to 1914 and 1946 respectively. It is an association of merchant banks, investment banks, securities firms and portfolio management companies, i.e. it excludes clearing banks and includes non-bank institutions which cannot, by legal definition, become members of the BBA. Membership is also open to merchant and investment banks that are subsidiaries of British clearing banks, as well as to foreign banks or branches that operate in the United Kingdom. Building societies, which have attained key significance as a category of financial institutions, are members of The Building Societies Association.

Smaller associations include the Association of British Consortium Banks, the London Discount Market Association, the Sterling Brokers' Association, the Foreign Exchange & Currency Deposit Brokers' Association and the International CD Market Association.

1989/90 saw the establishment, under the umbrella of the Securities and Investment Board (SIB), of five recognised self-regulatory organisations (SROs), which are also responsible for special supervisory functions on the basis of the Financial Services Act of 1988 and general rules established by the SIB. The SROs are The Association of Futures Brokers and Dealers Limited (AFBD) and The Securities Association (TSA), which have since merged to form the Securities and Futures Authority (SFA), and the Investment Management Regulatory Organisation (IMRO), the Financial Intermediaries, Managers and Brokers Regulatory Association (Fimbra) and the Life Insurance and Unit Trust Regulatory Organisation (Lautro). And finally, there are 'recognised professional bodies' (RPBs) for freelance portfolio management services.

7 *Ireland*

General outline

It was only in the 1960s that the banking system in Ireland really started to develop. In addition to the services it provided for private clients, it served to satisfy the needs of agriculture and small-scale industry. The currency union with the United Kingdom, which lasted for 150 years, was actually also a disincentive to a stronger development of the financial system in Ireland. This changed with the pursuit of a policy of increased industrialisation, with Ireland's accession – together with the United Kingdom and Denmark – to the European Economic Community in 1973, and, finally, with the country's membership of the European Monetary System, which resulted in the dissolution of the currency union with the United Kingdom.

Role of the Central Bank of Ireland

It was as early as 1971 that the adoption of the Central Bank Act created the legal foundations for a modern central bank that is responsible not only for the normal monetary policy functions but also for banking supervision. However, the autonomy it regained in the field of external and internal monetary policy is strictly limited. Formerly, the level of interest rates was determined by the rates in the United Kingdom and liquidity shortages or excesses were offset by free access to the market in London. Today, by contrast, the task of monetary policy is primarily to use interest and credit policy measures to keep the exchange rates stable within the scope of Ireland's EMS obligations, and thus indirectly to ensure domestic price stability. Since November 1989, all licensed banks have had to maintain a primary cash ratio of a uniform 10%, even though the reserve deposits at the Central Bank of Ireland only carry interest at a rate slightly below the market rates. This ratio has subsequently been lowered progressively since the beginning of 1991 until it reached 3% in early 1994. In September 1993, the range of financial institutions subject to this ratio was broadened to include both building societies and the two state development banks (both at a ratio of 3%).

Legislation, banking supervision and the market shares of the individual categories of banks

The legal foundations for the supervision of banks by the central bank date back to the Central Bank Act of 1971 (and a number of later amendments). The central bank developed various standards and behavioural rules, which it applied flexibly, partly without any express legal basis; finally, in 1989, these provisions were integrated into a new Central Bank Act. Banking business, which requires the issue of a licence, is defined relatively broadly; it includes deposit business as well as all traditional banking operations.

Until early 1989, the central bank supervised only one of four categories of banks, namely that of licensed banks.

However, that category's market share comes to 82% in terms of the aggregate balance sheet total of all banks, excluding the deposits of branches abroad, or to some 70% in terms of all non-bank deposits. Building societies have a market share of 13% (or 20% in terms of their clients' deposits), while the savings banks, including the Post Office Savings Bank, account for 3% (7%) and the public development banks for 2% (just under 4%). At the end of 1989, the consolidated balance sheet total of all Irish banks came to I£34.9 billion (I£15.4 billion of which was accounted for by deposits of resident non-banks, and I£2.8 billion by deposits of non-residents).

Associated banks

The most important banking category within that of all licensed banks is that of the associated banks, which have a share of 47% in the balance sheet total of all credit institutions. It comprises four clearing banks (the term 'associated banks' dates back to the Central Bank Act of 1942 which had defined a special relationship between these four clearing banks and the central bank). Their market share, and thus the actual degree of concentration in the Irish banking system, is even higher if the consolidated balance sheet total of the four leading banking groups is used as a basis, because each clearing bank also has a merchant bank subsidiary and – with only one exception – an industrial banking subsidiary.

Two of the banking groups are of Irish origin, namely Allied Irish Banks Limited and Bank of Ireland. Ulster Bank Limited is a wholly-owned subsidiary of National Westminster Bank Limited in London. The fourth clearing bank, Northern Bank (Ireland) Limited, was taken over by National Australia Bank Limited in 1987. With the exception of the latter, the clearing banks all have extensive networks with a total of some 660 branch offices. The four clearing banks have a broad range of financial services on offer, either directly or via subsidiaries. Since 1985, every clearing bank has fixed its own lending rates on the basis of the trend in the money market rates.

Non-associated banks

All other licensed banks are what are known as 'non-associated banks'. The category encompasses 29 banks with a market share of 35%, distributed almost equally between 20 merchant and commercial banks, on the one hand, and 9 industrial banks for a variety of industrial, commercial and consumer loans, on the other. The banks involved are either subsidiaries of the four large clearing banks, subsidiaries of banks from North America, branches of other foreign (usually EU) banks and a few are of Irish origin. They are all specialised institutions, though many operate as part of a larger corporate group.

International links

A characteristic feature of the Irish banking system is the relatively strong influence of foreign banks. Conversely, only a few major (usually associated) banks have branch offices abroad, most of which are concentrated regionally in Great Britain and Northern Ireland. In addition, there are a number of branch offices in several other financial centres abroad.

Building societies

The core business of the nine building societies is the granting of mortgage loans for housing. All the building societies, except the one controlled by the Bank of Ireland, are mutual associations and similar to the building societies in the United Kingdom. Both the amounts paid up on members' shares and other deposits can be withdrawn at short notice. The provisions of the Building Societies Act of 1976 restricted the business of building societies to granting variable interest mortgage loans.

The legislative reforms initiated in 1986 saw the first steps towards a diversification of their business. The adoption of the Building Societies Act of 12 July 1989, which transferred the responsibility for supervising building societies from the Registrar of Building Societies to the central bank with effect from 1 September 1989, set the points in the direction of a further expansion of their business activities. 1 May 1990 saw the introduction of a system to protect both the amounts paid up on members' shares and savings deposits (a similar system for the banks had come into effect on 1 November 1989). At the end of 1989, the consolidated balance sheet total of all building societies came to I£4.5 billion, which corresponded to a market share of 13%.

Other financial institutions

At the end of 1989, the three savings banks had a market share worth only I£1.1 billion, or 3%. They are the Post Office Savings Bank, with 1400 branch offices, and two trustee savings banks. The latter were also subjected to banking supervision by the central bank in that year.

In addition, there are two public development banks that are legally classified banks, namely the Agricultural Credit Corporation Limited and the Industrial Credit Company Limited, both of which not only receive funds from the government but also raise an increasing proportion of their funding on the market.

In 1989, banking supervision by the central bank was extended to cover those institutions which do not operate as banks. These include the previously unsupervised finance companies established in the International Financial Services Centre (IFSC), the Irish Futures and Options Exchange (IFOX), which was established in May 1989, money brokers, and finally, any investment funds which meet the EU requirements for 'undertakings for collective investment in transferable securities' (UCITS).

Associations of the banking sector and their members

All banks licensed in Ireland are represented by the Irish Bankers' Federation. In addition, the four associated banks have a representative body of their own, namely the Irish Banks' Standing Committee. The Association of International Banks represents the interests of the foreign banks, while the industrial banks and finance companies are members of the Irish Finance Houses Association. And finally, there is the Financial Services Industry Association within the Confederation of Irish Industry which represents the interests of suppliers of financial services at that level.

8 Denmark

General outline

1 October 1988 saw the abolition of the last controls on international capital transactions. The opening-up of the domestic market to competitors from abroad did not, however, have any major impact on the internationalisation of the Danish banking sector. All in all, the process of deregulation was actually to the detriment of foreign banks, especially after the abolition of quantitative credit controls in 1985. Conversely, the leading Danish banks sharply expanded their networks of branch offices abroad in the late 1980s. However, heavy losses both in Denmark and abroad resulted in some retrenchment in the early 1990s.

The universal banks were able to diversify their operations considerably. Fostered by appropriate legislation, it was primarily the sparekasser *(savings banks) that were able to make up some ground on the leading* banker *(banks), but the formerly strict distinction between banks (including savings banks),* realkreditinstitutter *(mortgage banks) and insurance companies has likewise been eased somewhat. The capital interlinks between these three categories have increased perceptibly. Recently, the banking environment has been marked by spectacular bank mergers, which have led to a further increase in the already relatively high degree of concentration. The universal banks continued to endeavour to improve their earnings by implementing large-scale balance sheet restructuring and rationalisation measures.*

Structure and functions of the Danmarks Nationalbank

Under the provisions of the Act of 7 April 1936, Danmarks Nationalbank is responsible, as the central bank, for maintaining a healthy currency system, for facilitating and regulating payments and for supervising lending operations. Responsibility for actual banking supervision, however, is vested in the Supervisory Office for the Finanstilsynet (financial services sector), a body subordinate to the Ministry of Industry. In addition to its monetary and credit policy tasks, Danmarks Nationalbank in Copenhagen is responsible for implementing the exchange rate policy co-ordinated with the government and for the issue of banknotes; it is also the government's banker and fiscal agent. In 1975, it took over the Royal Mint from the Ministry of Finance and has since then also been responsible for the issue of coins. Since 1936, when it was transformed from a public limited company into a foundation, Danmarks Nationalbank has had the status of an independent institution and enjoys a high degree of formal autonomy. The Minister of Finance and the Royal Bank Commissioner, or their deputies, are entitled to take part in the negotiations of the Board of Governors on the fixing of the discount rate and the rate of interest on cash advances, but without having the right to vote. In fact, however, the relationship between the central bank and the government is marked by a high degree of co-operation.

The Board of Governors consists of three members who are appointed for an indefinite period (the Governor by the Crown, i.e. the Government, and the two other members by the Board of Directors). It is responsible for formulating both monetary and credit policy, taking all decisions after consultations with the ministers responsible for economic policy, as well as for the day-to-day management of the bank. Another significant fact is that the Minister of Economic Affairs is also the Royal Bank Commissioner responsible for monitoring that the central bank fulfils its statutory tasks. In addition, a characteristic of the way monetary policy is pursued is that, in many cases, monetary policy objectives are implemented on the basis of 'voluntary' agreements concluded between the central bank and the Danish Banking Association. The Board of Governors is assisted by the Board of Directors, which has 25 members, and by its seven-member Committee of Directors.

Together with the abolition of credit controls, 1985 also saw the introduction of a rather more market-oriented system of controlling bank liquidity and influencing the money market rates. It was based on the issue of certificates of deposit by the central bank. In case of need, the banks could sell the certificates back to the central bank, or use them as a basis for short term loans.

After a lengthy period of experimentation, the central bank decided in July 1989 to grant banks current account credit at any time, subject to their providing Lombard collateral in the form of publicly quoted bonds. An alternative, however, were one-day securities repurchase agreements, which were automatically extended from day to day unless the central bank decided otherwise. Since November 1989, the interest rate on such loans has been a uniform 1% higher than the rate paid by the central bank on current account balances. January 1988 saw the revocation of a system of special deposits at the central bank in the order of 20% of any increase in excess of a basic rate of 7% in the client deposits carried by the banks.

Since April 1992, the banks have had virtually no further access to central bank overnight credit. Although the banks can overdraw their accounts heavily during the day, all accounts must be balanced daily at 3.30 pm sharp. In addition, the practice of banks to deposit surpluses at interest at the central bank were restricted sharply. Instead, the central bank offers the banks short term certificates of deposit with maturities of 14 days at weekly intervals, in which they are to invest any excess liquidity. Such certificates can be traded only between the central bank and the banks (the buying rate being 0.1% higher than the selling rate), and are thus an instrument intended for the interbank money market. Whenever necessary, the central bank can provide the banks with liquidity via repurchase agreements involving either treasury bills or government bonds. Only in exceptional cases will the central bank intervene directly in the market for treasury bills, or act as lender in the money market.

The key intermediate monetary policy target is no longer the money stock M2 – which includes non-banks' stocks of treasury bills and which has recently risen faster than the nominal gross national product – but rather the maintenance of that interest rate differential *vis-à-vis* Deutsche Mark interest rates that is necessary to ensure that the exchange rates in the EMS remain stable.

Legislation and banking supervision

Since 1975, upon the entry into force of the *Bank Loven* (Banking Act) of 2 April 1974, plus later amendments, both commercial and savings banks have had the same status in all major fields, such as the banking business they are permitted to conduct and the banking supervisory provisions applicable to them. Only these banks may accept deposits from the general public. For a long time, the key difference between the two types of banks was that only the commercial banks were organised in the form of public limited companies, and thus able to raise new capital via the stock market, while the savings banks were *selvejende institutioner*; independent non-profit institutions similar to foundations in character.

The reform of the Banking Act at the end of 1988 enabled savings banks, too, to be converted into public limited companies. By the end of 1989, four of the larger savings banks, which accounted for more than 68% of all deposits in the savings bank sector, had already changed their legal status in this way. Similar legislation is planned with respect to mortgage banks, which are presently not deemed to be banks as defined in the Act. These changes in the law will allow the credit institutions to expand their business activities by establishing financial holding companies. This possibility has resulted in insurance companies, too, entering the fields of investment consultancy and real estate agent services, or to their becoming active in the automobile leasing business.

The Supervisory Office for Financial Services, which is responsible for supervising both commercial and savings banks, has extended its scope of activities considerably in the last few years. After it had taken charge of the supervision of investment companies and credit co-operatives in 1983 and 1985, respectively, the supervision of insurance companies was merged with that of banks in 1988. A corresponding amendment of the Act on Mortgage Banks moreover provided for responsibility for the supervision of such institutions to be transferred from the Ministry of Housing to the Ministry of Industry.

Market shares of the individual categories of banks

At the end of 1989, the balance sheet total of all banks came to DKr 1076 billion, three-quarters of which

(DKr 790 billion) was accounted for by the commercial banks, and the remaining quarter by the savings banks. The *andelskasser* (credit co-operatives) had deposits totalling DKr 2.2 billion, and were thus of virtually no significance. At that time, there were more than 200 independent banking institutions in Denmark; they had a total of 3400 branch offices and 50 000 employees, i.e. they accounted for about 3.6% of all wage and salary earners. This proportion is far higher than in the other Scandinavian countries, or in Switzerland. This was probably the decisive reason why early 1990 saw the establishment of two big banks through two three-way mergers, which were aimed expressly at closing roughly one-quarter of all branch offices and at bringing about considerable rationalisation effects.

Leading universal banks

At the end of 1989 the largest bank, with a market share of 35% and a balance sheet total of DKr 377 billion, was Den Danske Bank. It resulted from a merger of the earlier institution of the same name with the Copenhagen Handelsbank and the Provinsbanken. Slightly smaller than Den Danske Bank is the second big bank, Unibank, which had a market share of 26.5% and a balance sheet total of DKr 284 billion. It resulted from the merger of three institutions, namely SDS (formerly the largest savings bank), Privatbanken and Andelsbanken. In addition to these two dominant banks, there are two medium-sized banks which likewise have country-wide networks of branch offices, namely Sparekassen Bikuben savings bank (with a market share of 6.7%) and Jyske Bank (with a market share of 5.9%). The four largest institutions thus accounted for almost three-quarters of the total business volume.

The other banks are only of regional or local significance. Since 1989, quite a number of them have merged either with one another (Varde Bank and Aktivbanken are now part of Sydbank Sønderjylland) or with one of the four big banks (Sparekassen Sydjylland joined Bikuben). Competitors which must also be considered in the field of deposits, however, are the insurance companies, pension funds, mortgage banks and, albeit to a lesser degree, foreign banks.

The liberalisation of access to the stock exchange in Copenhagen has led to the establishment of a large number of broking firms which are owned by commercial banks, savings banks and insurance companies. At the end of 1989, 22 of 38 broking firms were controlled by domestic financial institutions, and six by institutions from abroad. Both domestic and foreign banks are now entitled to have direct access to the stock exchange.

Danish banks abroad

At the end of 1989, the network of establishments abroad maintained by Danish banks consisted of 15 subsidiaries and a further 45 branch offices, 24 of which were mere offices without significant staff numbers in the Cayman Islands, but this number has been cut significantly since. Other focal points of business operations were in London, Luxembourg and Singapore. Half of the business involved was conducted with offices in Denmark.

Mortgage banks

Denmark's mortgage banks are of great significance. At the end of 1989, the volume of mortgage loans outstanding totalled DKr 739 billion. It was thus twice as high as the volume of government bonds outstanding. There were five such institutions (which has since risen to eight), three of which (now six normal institutions) grant mortgage loans to finance housing construction or other projects, while two specialise in mortgages on industrial and agricultural land. So far, these institutions have been organised either as *selvejende institutioner*, i.e. autonomous non-profit undertakings in which nobody actually owns an institution's assets, or as 'borrowers' credit co-operatives whose members are their respective borrowers.

A peculiarity of Danish mortgage banks which are organised as credit co-operatives is that borrowers are jointly and severally liable – up to the value of the real estate mortgaged – for their institution's liabilities. Traditionally, joint and several liability was included in the capital base. In recent years, however, this has been gradually reduced, and the capital base has been eroded further by heavily publicised losses and provisions during the recession. The three additional mortgage banks founded fairly recently all have capital links to commercial banks. The two largest banks each maintain one such institution as a subsidiary, Danske Kredit and Unikredit respectively.

Another peculiarity of Danish mortgage banks, which is rooted in tradition, is that the mortgagers receive the mortgage loans in the form of mortgage bonds which they must sell at current market terms on the open bond market. The loan-to-value ratio in the case of single-family houses is in the range of 80% of the value of the real estate. The terms and conditions governing the loans are determined by the purpose for which they are intended. Fixed-interest mortgage loans granted to finance single-family houses, for instance, may run for up to 30 years.

Other specialised institutions

In addition to the mortgage banks, there are a number of other specialised institutions, the capital of which is held by banks, insurance companies or industrial enterprises, and which refinance themselves on the capital market.

They grant medium term loans to finance investment in industry, the crafts and shipping. This closes the gap between rather short term bank lending and long term mortgage loans. Danish exports receive financial support either directly from the Danish Export Financing Corporation or indirectly in the form of export guarantees granted by the Danish Export Credit Council.

Associations of the banking sector and their members

The most important body representing the interests of banks in Denmark *vis-à-vis* the government, parliament, the central bank and the public in general was traditionally Den Danske Bankenforening (Danish Banking Association). It played a key role in monetary policy agreements with the central bank. A separate representative body of the savings banks was the Danmarks Sparkasse Forening, which merged with Den Danske Bankenforening in 1990 to form the Finansrådet. The smaller commercial and savings banks with their headquarters outside Copenhagen have joined forces in the Forening af Lokale Pengeinstitutter, formerly the De Danske Provinsbankers Forening.

9 Italy

General outline

Italy was one of the founder members of the European Community. However, its banking system differs in several respects from the more universal systems in central and western Europe, which are geared more strongly to competition and free flows of money and capital. Compared with the systems in the three other southern European countries, i.e. Spain, Portugal and Greece, which joined the EC much later, structural change in Italy has been particularly rapid in more recent years.

The severe economic crisis in the 1930s was reflected in the Banking Act of 1936, the core provisions of which were aimed at ensuring stability and security and which was still applicable until very recently. Strictly speaking, the 1936 legislation was only replaced by the new Banking Act of 1 September 1993, which came into force on 1 January 1994. However, the new law incorporates quite a number of legislative and administrative changes effected since 1990, to bring Italian banking regulations into line with what is the norm in the European Union. After the adoption of the Legge Amato *on 30 July 1990, the next milestone was the guidelines of November 1990 on the establishment of credit groups, which permitted public banks to reorganise themselves as joint stock companies. This was followed by the translation into Italian national law of the Second EC Banking Directive in December 1992 which made universal banking a permissible form of organisation in Italy, even though the choice of the organisational form tends to be driven rather more by strategic or fiscal considerations than by prudential requirements. Then the political decision was taken in May 1993 to allow banks to acquire participating interests in industrial companies up to the limit of 15% of their own funds.*

The leading credit institutions are under the direct or indirect control of the government. What is known as party political lottizzazione *(patronage) has increased the influence of the government and fostered the development of a certain bureaucratic character in these banks. Initially, the Banking Act of 1936 was based on a system of single-purpose banks, in which standard credit institutions were permitted only to conduct short term deposit and lending business as well as securities business on behalf of third parties, and prohibited the acquisition of participating interests in industrial enterprises. Medium and long term loans with maturities of more than 18 months could be granted only by specialised institutions.*

The structure of banking in Italy has since moved increasingly away from that initial situation. Competition among the various credit institutions and changes in the relevant banking supervision provisions, primarily in the late 1980s, have initiated a process of diversification, which has been accompanied, however to a certain degree, by a trend towards respecialisation.

Today, for instance, all standard credit institutions, including the savings banks, no longer need any special authorisation by the Banca d'Italia to grant medium and long term loans, provided that their total does not exceed a certain proportion of their capital and remains below the ceiling of 15% of the funds deposited with a given institution. On the basis of a concept of multi-functional groups, at any rate, they are able to grant such loans via special subsidiaries and can thereby also move to near-banking business, such as leasing and factoring services. Appropriate agreements concluded between banks, specialised credit institutions and insurance companies provide for the marketing of the financial products of other institutions. The administrative controls and regulations on the investment of funds in government securities have gradually been revoked since 1984.

Both that and the ground gained by newly-introduced certificates of deposit have led to sharper competition and a closer orientation of debit and credit interest rates to the money market rates, so that the previously relatively high interest margins have come under pressure. In addition, the Italian central bank has fostered competition, by encouraging mergers of smaller credit institutions and, since May 1990, by discontinuing its policy of limiting and controlling the expansion of branch networks by demanding evidence of the economic necessity for such an expansion. The abolition of the last exchange controls shortly before the commencement of the first stage of the Economic and Monetary Union on 1 July 1990, as well as the increased presence of foreign banks, has given a new impetus to the internationalisation of the Italian banking system.

Recently, banks have also been permitted to acquire participating interests in merchant banks, securities houses and insurance companies. It has been decided to convert the public law banks step-by-step into public limited companies and to reduce the government's equity capital holdings from the present 100% to 51%, with that share perhaps being held via a financial holding company.

Structure and functions of the Banca d'Italia

The Banca d'Italia, a public law institution which has its head office in Rome, fulfils the functions of the Italian banking system's central bank, is the bank of issue and the government's principal banker. It is responsible not only for the implementation of monetary policy and banking supervision but also, together with the Ufficio Italiano dei Cambi (Italian Foreign Exchange Office), for exchange rate policy. The governor, who is appointed by the Council of Ministers, has a relatively independent status as removal from office is not provided for. However, it is the Comitato Interministeriale per il Credito e il Risparmio (CICR; Interministerial Committee on Credit and Savings), which comprises the Minister of the Treasury and other ministers responsible for economic policy issues, with the governor of the central bank attending meetings only in an advisory capacity, that issues general directives in respect of not only internal and external monetary policy but also banking supervision policy and that must also approve the central bank's credit policy proposals.

The position held by the Minister of Finance is even stronger than that of the chairman of the CICR. It is the Minister of Finance who is responsible, together with the Minister of Trade, for all foreign exchange policy decisions, for instance, and who appoints or dismisses the presidents of public banks in consultation with the political parties. Although the central bank has no longer been required, since an agreement reached with the Minister of Finance in 1981, to automatically take over any government securities placed on the market into its portfolio, the government made constant use of the cash advance facility in the order of up to 14% of its projected budgetary expenditure before the Maastricht rules came into effect in 1994. Authority to determine the discount rate was transferred from the Minister of Finance to the central bank in February 1992. In January 1994, the central bank also assumed responsibility for determining minimum reserve policy.

For purposes of achieving the envisaged goal of internal monetary stability as well as other economic policy objectives, the central bank defines several monetary intermediate targets each year, such as the desired growth of either bank lending or the extended money stock M2. In recent years, particularly since Italy decided at the beginning of 1990 to keep to the narrower margin of fluctuation provided for under EMS rules, the stability of the exchange rate *vis-à-vis* the currencies of EMS partner countries, especially with the Deutsche Mark, came to the fore. In that context, minimum reserve policy and open market operations were used to ensure that the interest rate differential to the Deutsche Mark narrowed only to such an extent that a weakening of the lira on the exchange markets appeared avoidable. That restraint became less tight in September 1992 when Italy, together with the United Kingdom, saw itself compelled to withdraw completely from the EMS exchange rate mechanism and to devalue the lira so as to regain the initiative on the financial markets.

The central bank has gradually been easing up on its minimum reserve requirements since October 1990. Up to 5% of the required minimum reserves may be mobilised (as from October 1991) for payment purposes, so that they do not have to be maintained at the required level from day to day, but only on average each month. 1991 saw a change in the basic minimum reserves to the benefit of the banking sector. Although the foreign currency deposits of residents were subjected to minimum reserve requirements, the funds which the banks raise through borrowing abroad (net) and via repurchase agreements were completely exempt from such requirements.

Legislation and banking supervision

At the end of 1989, the structure of the Italian banking system was still determined predominantly by the Banking Act of 1936, which consisted of a whole range of legislative initiatives adopted between 1936 and 1938: The underlying approach, namely a strict regulation of credit institutions' deposit and lending business, together with far-reaching discretionary powers for the Banca d'Italia (as the key banking supervisory body) and the Minister of Finance, had been retained, despite a number of reforms implemented in the 1980s.

The Banking Act of 1936 divides credit institutions into two major categories, namely into *aziende di credito ordinario* (standard credit institutions), the core business of which, even today, is short term lending (for periods of up to 18 months), and specialised credit institutions which are responsible for granting medium and long term loans. Banking supervision covers all undertakings that conduct banking business; this includes the acceptance of deposits of money, irrespective of their form, and taking in debt securities, to the extent that the funds involved are used for lending.

Structure of the banking sector and the market shares of the standard credit institutions

At the end of 1989, there were 1085 standard credit institutions with a network of 15 577 domestic branch offices and some 318 000 employees (see Table 5). Through the elimination of geographic restrictions as a result of the revocation of the requirement to submit evidence of economic necessity (*de facto* as from March 1989, but legally only as from May 1990), banks were able to extend their branch networks solely on the basis of their individual marketing strategies, and the number of branch offices increased by 130 in 1989 alone. Milan is the most important financial centre, even though both the government and the central bank are situated in Rome.

The directives of the CICR of January 1989 allow electronic payment systems, too, to be extended as needed. At the end of 1989, there were some 13000 self-service banking machines (ATMs), as well as about 13000 point-of-sale terminals.

The Banking Act distinguishes between several legal categories of standard credit institutions, namely between public law credit institutions, banks of national interest, big banks, credit co-operatives, savings banks, pawnbroking institutions, agricultural and artisans' cash offices, and branches of all types of foreign credit institutions (for the Italian terms, see Table 5).

Public law credit institutions

At the end of 1989, the top category encompassed six public law credit institutions with a network of 2236 branch offices, a one-fifth share of domestic deposit business and major participating interests both in other banks and in the near-banking field, including leasing, factoring and merchant banking. The institutions involved were Banca Nazionale del Lavoro (BNL), Banco di Napoli, Istituto Bancario San Paolo di Torino, Monte dei Paschi di Siena, Banco di Sicilia and Banco di Sardegna. While Istituto Bancario San Paolo di Torino and Monte dei Paschi di Siena (a foundation) both had a strong capital base, the other institutions suffered from undercapitalisation.

This was the most important reason why all public law institutions were to be given the opportunity, as outlined in the *Legge Amato* of 30 July 1990, to be transformed into public limited companies. Another reason was to prepare the ground for their eventual privatisation at a later stage. Irrespective of the fact that banking business is still concentrated on short term lending and deposit transactions, the public law credit institutions now conduct a whole range of typical banking and near-banking operations, but often via subsidiaries. In recent times, they have been taking a particular interest (as have a number of other

Table 5 *Structure of the Italian banking system[1] (at the end of 1989)*

Types of banks, broken down by legal category	Number of banks	Branch offices	Domestic client deposits	Equity capital[6]
			In lire trillion	
Istituto di credito di diritto pubblico	6	2 236	118.0	16.1
Banche di interesse nazionale	3	1 280	68.7	11.1
Banche di credito ordinario[2]	110	3 519	149.6	19.6
Banche popolari cooperative	113	2 834	108.8	16.1
Casse di risparmio	75	4 032	175.6	22.6
Monti di credito su pegno di la 1 a categoria[3]	7	166		
Monti di credito su pegno di la 2 a categoria[3]	2	6	...	...
Casse rurali e artigiane	728	1 446	4.0[4]	0.5[4]
Filiali di banche estere	36	53	...	...
Istituti di categoria[5]	5	5	0.6	1.6
Total	**1085**	**15 577**	**624.8**	**85.9**

Source: Banca d'Italia, Assemblea Generale Ordinaria dei Participanti, Appendice (1989 Annual Report).

1 Excluding specialised credit institutions and finance companies (including merchant banks).

2 Public limited companies plus one private limited company and the Banca Nazionale delle Communicazioni.

3 'Pledge banks'.

4 Major agricultural cash offices.

5 Central credit institutions.

6 For banking supervision purposes.

major banks) in insurance business, an interest that is not only reflected in national and international agreements on the marketing of insurance products, but that has in a number of cases also led to the acquisition of considerable participating interests in insurance companies.

In 1986, for instance, BNL (the largest Italian bank) established an insurance subsidiary, Lavoro Vita, the products of which are marketed – together with other lending, saving and insurance products – by the 1220 or so agents of Interbancaria. BNL has a capital holding of 30% in Interbancaria, while the public insurance company INA (which, in turn, holds 20% of BNL's capital) and Banco di Sicilia have participating interests of 21% and 18% respectively. Istituto Bancario San Paolo di Torino co-operates with Guardian Royal Exchange (a British insurance company, which has majority stakes in two Italian property insurance companies) and has a majority interest in Polaris Vita, a life insurance company.

Reciprocal capital links with insurance companies have also recently been on the increase in the rest of the banking sector. In this context, the relatively large share of about one-quarter of total insurance business in Italy accounted for by foreign companies acted as a catalyst in the move towards one-stop financing strategies. RAS Bank, for instance, is a new commercial bank established jointly by Riunione Adriatica di Sicurita, the second-largest Italian insurance company, which is controlled in turn by the German Allianz Group.

The three 'big banks'

The three big banks – Banca Commerciale Italiana, Credito Italiano and Banco di Roma – are also pursuing multifunctional concepts, in which increasing importance is being attached not only to securities business but also to the marketing of insurance products, or the acquisition of participating interests in insurance companies. These banks are public limited companies and maintain 1280 branch offices throughout the country. Their respective shares are traded on the stock exchange, but a government holding company, Istituto per la Ricostruzione Industriale (IRI), has majority holdings in them. However, the government has indicated its intention to change the shape of these banks once again.

Where the marketing of insurance products is concerned, Banca Commerciale Italiana co-operates with the largest Italian insurance company, Assicurazione Generali, and their subsidiary Genercomit, whose agents play a major role. In 1989, Credito Italiano, together with its sales subsidiary Mediofin, concluded an agreement on close marketing co-operation with Commercial Union, a British insurance company, which views that agreement as part of an all-European marketing concept.

Other private credit institutions

The 110 other standard credit institutions, most of which are privately owned and which in the case of new establishments must have the legal form of public limited companies, have a market share of around 25%. A number of these institutions are relatively large and well-represented at both the national and regional levels, while others are of only local significance.

The largest institutions in this category are Banca Nationale dell'Agricoltura, Banco di Santo Spirito (which recently merged with Cassa di Risparmio di Roma), Banca Toscana, Credito Romagnolo, Banca Provinciale Lombarda, Banco Ambrosiano Veneto (recently established through a merger between Nuovo Banco Ambrosiano and Banca Cattolica del Veneto, and which has thus become the most important private bank in northern Italy), Banco Lariano, Istituto Bancario Italiano,

Banca d'America e d'Italia (long a subsidiary of Bank of America then sold to Deutsche Bank AG some years ago), Credito Commerciale, Banca San Paolo-Brescia and Credito Bergamosco.

Credit co-operatives

A key role is also played by the *banche populari cooperative*, the credit co-operatives. The number of such institutions has been on the decline for years, although the number of branch offices has been rising. Every member of such a credit co-operative has a vote. With the exception of Banca Populare di Novara and Banca Populare di Milano, the credit cooperatives are generally only of local or regional significance.

Savings banks and 'pledge banks'

About 30% of the deposits of resident clients of all credit institutions are carried by first-category savings banks and 'pledge banks'. They are either public law institutions or companies licensed by the Minister of Finance. As long as the capital reserves do not equal at least 10% of the deposits, profits are used primarily to build up such reserves, while 30% is used for charitable purposes. The savings banks and pawnbroking institutions, too, have become multifunctional banks. Since the reforms initiated at the beginning of the 1980s, they have been entitled to provide services similar to those of the commercial banks, and have also become active in international business. A peculiarity of the savings banks is that they have *sezioni di credito speciale* (special divisions for medium and long term business operations), which have capital but no legal personality of their own.

By far the largest savings bank, which – measured in terms of the total volume of deposits – is also the third-largest bank in Italy, is the Cassa di Risparmio delle Provincie Lombarde (Cariplo). It also has branches, participating interests and representative offices abroad. Savings banks of significant regional importance are the Cassa di Risparmio di Torino, the Cassa di Risparmio de Verona, Vicenza e Belluna, the Cassa di Risparmio Vittorio Emmanuele per le Provincie Siciliane and the Cassa di Risparmio di Firenze.

Rural and artisans' banks

Of lesser significance in terms of both their capital and deposits are the more than 700 rural and artisans' banks, most of which operate in the form of credit co-operatives to finance agriculture and the crafts and which may use only 25% of their deposits (which totalled L 38 trillion at the end of 1988) for lending to non-members.

Central institutions of the categories of banks

There are five central institutions of the individual categories of banks, which obtain most of their funding through interbank business and predominantly function as clearing and services centres for the respective categories of banks. They are the Istituto Centrale delle Casse di Risparmio Italiane (ICCRI) for the savings banks, the Istituto Centrale delle Casse Rurali e d'Artigiane (ICCREA) for the rural and artisans' banks, as well as Istituto delle Banche Populari, Istituto di Banche e Banchieri and Federalcasse.

Foreign credit institutions in Italy

At an estimated 3%, foreign credit institutions in Italy have a very limited share of the market. At the end of 1989, there were 36 such institutions, which maintained a total of 53 branch offices and concentrated on corporate business. In 1986, the Deutsche Bank AG acquired one of the largest private banks, Banca d'America e d'Italia, from Bank of America. Citibank is represented in central and southern Italy by Banca Centrosud, formerly a subsidiary of Banco di Roma.

Specialised credit institutions and specialised divisions for longer term lending

Medium and long term lending is the business of 54 specialised credit institutions, including the special divisions of a number of standard credit institutions, which have been subject to banking supervision by, but not to, the minimum reserve requirements of the Banca d'Italia since 1981. Their total lending, about 80% of the consolidated balance sheet total, came to some L 208 trillion at the end of 1988.

Istituto Mobiliare Italiano (IMI) provides industry with one-third of its longer term loans, is involved in the financing of development aid, of exports and imports and of investment in southern Italy, and obtains its funding not only on the capital market but also from banks and the public budget. Until 1981, Banca di Credito Finanziario (Mediobanca), which has recently been largely privatised, was the only merchant bank entitled to conduct business involving the issue of shares and the acquisition of participating interests in industry. Since that time, other specialised credit institutions have likewise been permitted, to a limited extent, to acquire stakes in industry. It was only in 1987 that merchant banks were licensed in general.

Other major institutions are Efibanca, Interbanca, Banca Centrale di Credito Populare and Mediocredito

Centrale as well as regional development banks, such as ISVEIMER, IRFIS and Credito Industriale Sardo, the financial business of which is in part limited to certain sectors and regions. Responsibility for export credit guarantees is vested in SACE, a special division of Istituto Nazionale per le Assicurazione (INA). Some 20 Istituti di Credito Fondario conduct long term mortgage business, as do the public law banks and special divisions of a number of other standard credit institutions.

Finance companies

In addition, there are numerous finance companies that engage in leasing, factoring and consumer credit business. Their equity capital is usually held by banks, but also by industrial enterprises and distribution companies. Their funding largely originates in the banking sector. Of key significance since an appropriate decision was taken by the CICR in February 1987 is that not only domestic and foreign banks but also insurance companies and other enterprises have been permitted to acquire participating interests in newly-established merchant banks, or *società di intermediazione finanziaria* (SIF).

In addition to providing advice and support in connection with corporate finance, a merchant bank is entitled to perform operations to procure both equity and debt capital as well as, in particular, to take over shares and bonds of enterprises up to their final placement. However, the total value of a SIF's participating interests must not exceed its equity capital, and that of a single participating interest is limited to 20% of its equity capital. Moreover, the participating interests must all remain minority holdings. In addition, the last few years have also seen a major expansion in the business of investment funds and portfolio management companies.

Associations of the banking sector and their members

By far the most important banking association is the Associazione Bancaria Italiana (ABI), which has its headquarters in Rome. Its membership comprises not only standard credit institutions but also specialised credit institutions, finance companies and leasing companies. The ABI fosters agreements between its members and represents their interests *vis-à-vis* the government, parliament and the central bank. Similarly comprehensive functions on behalf of the savings banks are fulfilled by the Associazione tra le Casse di Risparmio Italiane, which also has its seat in Rome. Other banking associations are the Associazione Nazionale Aziende Ordinarie di Credito (which does not include the big banks) in Milan, as well as the Associazione Nazionale Luigi Luzzotti tra le Banche Populari and the Associazione Tecnico delle Banche Populari Italiane, which both have their headquarters in Rome. The hundreds of small rural and artisans' banks are represented by the Federazione Italiana delle Casse Rurali e d'Artiziane which likewise has its headquarters in Rome. In addition to functioning as central giro institutions for the respective category of credit institution affiliated to them, the five aforementioned central institutions also represent the interests of these credit institutions.

10 Spain

General outline

The foundations for the modern Spanish financial system were laid by the new Ley de Ordenación del Crédito y de la Banca *(Banking Act) of 14 April 1962. But it was not until the 1970s and 1980s, especially after the accession of Spain to the European Community on 1 June 1986, that the most significant decisions were taken to pave the way both for an internationally competitive universal banking system and for the implementation of the single European market at the beginning of 1993. The policy pursued was marked by gradual deregulation and liberalisation, with the individual measures involved nevertheless tending to have far-reaching implications, by the granting of equal status to all domestic banks and by the licensing of foreign banks. Existing credit institutions became ever more universal in respect of their functions. This was not impaired by the establishment of numerous new specialised institutions, usually as parts of financial conglomerates.*

The Spanish banks enjoyed enormous rates of growth and sharp increases in profits in the 1980s and early 1990s. The key factors behind this fact were persistently favourable business activity at home, significant pent-up demand for financial services and limited competition within the banking sector.

Structure and functions of the Banco de España

The tasks of the Banco de España were defined unequivocally in a statutory regulation, of June 1962, on its nationalisation and reorganisation. Hierarchically and functionally, it remained fully dependent on the government. It was not until the adoption of the new Law of the Governing Body of the Banco de España on 21 June 1980 (Law No. 30) that it was granted a greater degree of autonomy. Further major changes occurred after the autonomy law entered into force on 3 June 1994.

The Banco de España is a public law entity with a legal character of its own. The central bank acts independently of the public administration in the pursuit of its goals. Although it was required, on the basis of the law of June 1980, to fulfil the general objectives set by the government in the implementation of its monetary policy, it was free to choose whatever monetary policy instruments it deemed appropriate for its purposes. The central bank's supreme decision-making body was the General Council which had fifteen members. In addition to implementing monetary policy, it is responsible for the banknotes in circulation, it functions as the government's principal banker and the bankers' bank, is involved in payments, holds the country's monetary reserves and is involved in cross-border payments, i.e. responsible for compliance with any capital controls still in force. It is also the banking supervisory authority. Since 1990, it has also conducted direct business (including the management of accounts) with the general public in connection with the issue of government securities.

Under the accepted EU commitments, all restrictions on cross-border capital transactions had to be abolished by the end of 1992, at the close of the transitionary period. Spain has been a member of the EMS since June 1989, and participates in the exchange rate mechanism, albeit initially only within a wider margin of ±6% *vis-à-vis* the currencies of the other partner countries and later – since the currency turbulences of July/August 1993 – within that of ±15%, as generally agreed between all remaining participants in the exchange rate mechanism.

In line with the provisions of a ministerial regulation of 21 February 1990, the central bank lowered the minimum reserves to be maintained by all credit institutions subject to the minimum reserve requirements from 17% to 5% so as to improve the international competitiveness of the Spanish institutions. The banks were required to invest the difference between these two percentages in central bank certificates of deposit at 6% interest, which are to be redeemed continuously – as from March 1993, in line with the increase in the minimum reserves anticipated as a result of the growth of deposits – up to the year 2000. The basic minimum reserves in the order of 5% of all deposits subject to minimum reserves requirements must be held free of interest at the central bank. In December 1992, this ratio was reduced further to 3%. The former obligation of banks to hold a certain percentage of their deposits in the form of low-interest treasury bonds was gradually cut to 11% from as early as February 1987, and was finally abolished at the end of 1992.

In the event of the credit institutions lacking an adequate supply of suitable government securities, they are entitled to use the newly created *Certificados del Banco de España* (Cebes; central bank paper) for open market operations in the form of securities repurchase agreements. With the introduction of the new regime of minimum reserve requirements, the usual daily auction was replaced by ten-day auctions as the most important monetary policy instrument of directly influencing short term money market rates. Daily auctions are now used solely for fine-tuning purposes, and are carried out, whenever necessary, with a limited number of *creadores de mercado* (market makers).

The main intermediate target of monetary policy is the money stock *activos liquidos en maños del publico* (ALP), which comprises not only M3 but also short term bank bonds and treasury bills. Since Spain's accession to the EMS, both the exchange rates and the interest rate differential *vis-à-vis* the other EMS currencies, above all the Deutsche Mark, have likewise played a major role.

The aforementioned autonomy law of June 1994 gave the Banco de España far-reaching independence from the government in all monetary policy matters aimed at attaining the final goal of price stability, even though it has to support the government's general economic policy. The government continues to be responsible for exchange rate policy, but must consult the Governor of the Banco de España before taking any decisions, which must moreover be compatible with the goal of price stability. Direct loans to the public sector are no longer possible. The main policy-making body is now the ten-member Consejo de Gobierno (Governor's Council), which consists of the Governor, the Deputy Governor, the Director-General of the Treasury (who has no vote in monetary policy matters), the Vice-President of the official Stock Exchange Commission (likewise without a vote) and six further *Consejos* (counsellors), who are appointed by the government. The Comision Ejecution (Executive Committee) is a managing body of four members, consisting of the Governor, the Deputy Governor and two full-time counsellors.

Banco de España as the banking supervisory authority, and other supervisory bodies

Banco de España is responsible for supervising all credit institutions, including (since July 1988) all specialised credit institutions and public law banks. Responsibility for the supervision of brokers and dealers in securities, of banks' securities business and of investment companies is still vested in the Comisión Nacional del Mercado de Valores, while insurance companies and investment funds are supervised by the Ministry of Economic Affairs.

Market shares of the individual categories of banks

At the end of 1989, there were 747 credit institutions with a combined balance sheet total equivalent to US$716 billion and more than 33 000 banking outlets. 341 of these institutions, which accounted for 91% of that balance sheet total, belonged to the four narrowly defined categories of banks, the *bancos privados* (private commercial banks), the *cajas de ahorro* (savings banks), the *entidades oficiales de crédito* (public banks) and the *cooperativas de crédito* (credit co-operatives), which had shares of 51.7%, 27.9%, 9.2% and 2.3% respectively, in the combined balance sheet total. With only a few exceptions, the institutions in these categories are all universal banks.

The remaining 9% of the credit institutions' combined balance sheet total was accounted for by manifold specialised credit institutions, such as *sociedades de crédito hipotecario* (mortgage banks; 0.7%), *entidades de arrendamiento financiero* (leasing companies; 6.2%), *entidades de financiación* (finance companies; 1.8%), eight discount houses and financial intermediaries active in the money market. Most of these institutions are affiliated to larger domestic and foreign universal banks.

Other financial institutions in a broader sense outside the banking sector are insurance companies and pension funds, factoring companies, securities dealers and investment companies. In this sector, too, capital links to the major private commercial banks have recently been on the increase.

Private commercial banks

Within the group of 146 private commercial banks, the distinctions between *bancos comerciales* and *bancos industriales*, as had formerly been prescribed by legislators but which have since been largely revoked, are of only minor significance today. Measured in terms of the balance sheet total at the end of 1989, about half the business was accounted for by only seven big banks. These were: Banco Bilbao Vizcaya (BBV), which had a balance sheet total of US$51.5 billion and which resulted from a merger between Banco de Bilbao (the oldest commercial bank in Spain, dating back to 1857) and Banco de Vizcaya; Banco Central with a balance sheet total of US$31.4 billion (it has since merged with Banco Hispaño-Americano and has been named Banco Central Hispaño-Americano); Banco de Santander with a balance sheet total of US$28.2 billion, which has since emerged as the first-ranking bank after a period of strong and profitable expansion and after recently acquiring a majority stake in the deficit-ridden Banco Español de Crédito (Banesto); Banco Hispaño Americano with a balance sheet total of US$27.3 billion (in which Commerzbank AG in Frankfurt had acquired a small minority stake and which, in turn, has many participating interests in specialised institutions, including one in Spain's third-largest insurance company); Banco Exterior de España with a balance sheet total of US$17.9 billion (in which the government has a majority holding of 51%); Banco Español de Crédito and Banco Popular.

The role played by these seven banks is greater than that suggested by the figures given, because they own not only many specialised banks but also a number of other supra-regional private banks, as well as regional and local banks. Calculated on a consolidated basis, the share of the seven big banks in the balance sheet total of all private commercial banks comes to well over four-fifths. The four largest independent regional and local banks at the time were Banco Pastor, Banco de Sabadell, Banco March and Banco Herrero.

The category of private banks has recently been enlarged by a number of modern merchant banks. Although several of these new establishments are owned by domestic banks, the main impetus came from abroad, in particular from foreign merchant and investment banks. As foreign banks are highly dependent on the national and international interbank markets in respect of their funding, many of these banks specialise in merchant banking and other innovative financial operations. This has resulted in a significant increase in competition in certain market segments.

Foreign banks in Spain and Spanish banks abroad

A total of 57 foreign banks conducted banking business in Spain at the end of 1989. 42 of these banks were represented by branch offices, and two by newly-established subsidiaries, while 13 were Spanish banks controlled by banks based abroad. Most of the branch offices were established on the basis of a Royal Decree (No. 1388) of 1978. Before that, there were already four foreign banks not covered by the provisions of that decree, namely Lloyds Bank, Crédit Lyonnais, Société Générale de Banque en Espagne and Banca Nazionale del Lavoro. Until the end of 1989 the licensing procedure used was relatively restrictive, with a limit of at most three branch offices per bank and the restriction of foreign banks' borrowing in Spain largely to the interbank market. These restrictions had been abolished by the end of 1992.

Measured in terms of the balance sheet total of all private commercial banks, which provides an inadequate picture of this category's relative importance, the branch offices of foreign banks alone had a market share of 6.5%. A number of subsidiaries of major foreign banks have branch office networks capable of extension. Deutsche Bank AG, for instance, had a majority stake in Comercial Transatlántico and took over another important regional bank, Banco de Madrid, in March 1993. The total share of foreign banks in business in Spain at the time was about 15%, but has since then been halved as a result of the strong expansion of business by the savings banks and some large private commercial banks.

Conversely, the establishment by Spanish banks of offices abroad, above all in other EU member states, had made little progress by the end of 1989. A bank that had proved to be remarkably active in this respect was the particularly profitable and innovative Banco de Santander, which had established reciprocal capital links with the Royal Bank of Scotland, with Banco de Comercio e Industria de Portugal and with Cariplo in Milan some time earlier.

Savings banks

The market share of the 79 savings banks, which are all foundations established by private or public entities, expanded significantly in the 1980s. Their strengths are to be found in the disproportionately sharp growth of private savings and time deposits, the volume of which has now almost reached that of the private commercial banks. By and large, the restrictions initially imposed on their business activities by the Savings Bank Act of 1933, one of which limited their operations to certain regions, have been abolished. The period from 1986 to 1989 alone saw the establishment of 1800 new branch offices. Today, the non-profit character of the savings banks is visible only in the use made of their profits, to the extent that such profits are not transferred in advance to the reserve fund of the savings banks. The autonomous government of the province in which a savings bank has its headquarters decides on the composition of its executive bodies, i.e. on that of the general assembly, the board of directors and the supervisory board which controls it.

To a certain degree, the Postal Savings Bank enjoys a special status. Although it has had the same status as the savings banks in lending business since the end of 1981, it must pass on half its profits to the government and is not a member of the savings banks' deposit guarantee fund. It is subordinate to the Minister of Transport, Tourism and Communications.

The degree of concentration in the savings bank sector is relatively marked. More than half of all deposits at the end of 1989 were carried by 10 savings banks. The largest savings bank is Caixa de Barcelona, which merged with another large savings bank, Caya de Pensiones, in 1991. The merger created a network of almost 220 branch offices and a total workforce of more than 11 000 employees. Next in size is Caya de Madrid, which has a balance sheet total of US$20 billion. The major savings banks are endeavouring to establish nationwide branch networks. In the last few years, some of them benefited from being able to take over a number of weak credit co-operatives. In interbank business, the savings banks have a structural creditor position *vis-à-vis* the private commercial banks. By tradition, lending by savings banks is concentrated on local authority loan business and on mortgage loans.

Credit co-operatives

The 111 credit co-operatives, most of which operate in rural areas, play only a modest role. Since 1988, only some of them have been affiliated to the central institution, Banco de Crédito Agricola (BCA). Subject to their meeting certain requirements, Banco de España may classify them as 'qualified credit co-operatives'. This gives them access to the rediscount credit facilities of the central bank, for instance, or allows them to issue certificates of deposit or to raise funds from public credit institutions. Another step towards universal banking business is marked by the possibility of lending to clients who are not members of the credit co-operative.

Official credit institutions

At the end of 1989, the category of official credit institutions comprised five institutions, the oldest of which, Banco Hipotecario de España, was established as long ago as 1872. As with three other institutions of this kind, namely Banco de Agricola, Banco de Crédito Industrial and Banco de Crédito Local, it is a public limited company, all shares of which have been owned by the government since the reforms of 1971. The institutions all grant longer term loans for purposes of key macroeconomic importance. The largest official credit institution, which is very special in character, however, is Banco Exterior Español, which was established in 1928, is governed by statutes of its own and was licensed by a ministerial order on 26 January 1972. Apart from carrying out all types of banking transactions in the same way as any private bank, it is responsible for granting official export credit and receives endowments for that purpose from the Instituto de Crédito Oficial (ICO).

The organisational and administrative structure of the official credit institutions was defined in Act No. 13 of 19 June 1971. The same year also marked the establishment of the Instituto de Crédito Oficial (ICO), an autonomous public law institution which became responsible solely for dealing with matters determined by the Ministry of Economic Affairs and Finance. With effect from 1 January 1988, the ICO acquired majority stakes in or took over the other four official credit institutions in full, as it did both the

Banco Exterior Español and the Postal Savings Bank at a later date. As a holding company, the ICO had the task of controlling and co-ordinating the activities of, and of passing on public funds to, the individual official credit institutions. In addition, the ICO was also given the right to raise funds from private sector sources, as has been the norm since 1988. In 1990, a co-operation agreement was concluded between, among others, the ICO and the German Kreditanstalt für Wiederaufbau. The ICO was later transformed into the holding company Argentaria, the third-largest credit institution in Spain, which operates as a kind of counterveiling power to the large private commercial banks. Half the public limited company's capital was transferred to private ownership in two stages in 1993 and early 1994.

Other specialised credit institutions

At the end of 1989 there were 126 leasing companies, which had a market share of 6.2% (as measured in terms of the balance sheet total of all credit institutions), and held a leading position within the category of specialised credit institutions. They have been subject to supervision by the central bank since 1988. A number of basic provisions are to be found in supplements No. 6 and No. 7 to Act No. 26 of 29 July 1988 on the structure and control of credit institutions. At 67% per annum, the rate of growth in leasing business was truly spectacular in the last three years before the end of 1989. Since 1 January 1990, universal banks have been permitted to conduct such business as well.

It was only through the adoption of Act No. 2 on the Mortgage Loan Market in 1981 that mortgage banks were licensed as specialised credit institutions. Provisions on the implementation of that Act are set out in Decree No. 685 of 1982. Eligible for licences are public limited companies that have equity capital totalling at least Pta 250 million. Loans secured by real estate liens are financed through the issue of bank bonds of various types, all of which are similar to mortgage bonds, through public deposits with terms of usually more than 18 months, and through interbank funds. The loans are granted to promote both the construction, maintenance and acquisition of housing and the improvement of the social infrastructure.

The market involved has been characterised by rapid growth for years. At the end of 1989, there were as many as 32 institutions, which accounted for as much as 6.4% of all mortgage lending. As mortgage banks – unlike the savings banks and other credit institutions engaged in mortgage business (except for Banco Hipotecario de España) – obtain their funding increasingly through the issue of bank bonds, their share in this form of raising finance came to 17.5% as early as the end of 1989.

Under the provisions of section 39 of Act No. 26 of 29 July 1988, *sociedades mediodoras del mercado de dinaro* (money market financial intermediaries) are now also counted among the credit institutions.

Associations of the banking sector and their members

The private commercial banks are represented by the Consejo Superior Bancario and by the Asociación Española de Banca Privada. The savings banks, including the Postal Savings Bank, are members of the Confederación Española de Cajas de Ahorros (CECA). Finance houses are the constituent members of the Representacion Española ante Eurofinas Comision Conjunta, while the credit co-operatives are members of the Union Nacional de Cooperativas de Crédito. All these banking associations have their headquarters in Madrid.

11 Portugal

General outline

The Portuguese banking system has been undergoing rapid change but only since the late 1980s. After the Salazar regime had been ousted, 1975 saw the nationalisation of all banks, with the exception of three foreign banks and all banks operating as credit co-operatives. In 1984, a cautious policy commenced allowing private capital once more to be used to conduct banking business, either through the establishment of new banks, which initially concentrated on investment banking, or through the partial reprivatisation of large commercial banks and depository institutions. On the increase since 1986 (the year in which Portugal, together with Spain, joined the European Community) has been, above all, the number of non-bank financial institutions which either offer only certain financial services or execute financial operations that the banks are not permitted to conduct.

These developments not only resulted in diversification that made the business of commercial banks even more similar to that of investment banks, but also led to an increase in the capital links between banks, on the one hand, and other credit institutions and insurance companies, on the other. They also provided capital from abroad with new opportunities, even though a fully free flow of capital within the single European market became possible only after the end of the extended period of transition, which eventually ended earlier than expected at the end of 1992. Even before that date, the admission of domestic and foreign private capital, together with other deregulation and liberalisation measures, had led to a significant increase in competition within the banking sector. September 1990 saw an amendment of the rules for the establishment of private banks on the basis of domestic or foreign capital. Among other things, private banks were induced to take over part of the nationalised banks' old loans at an agreed price.

Structure and functions of the Banco de Portugal

Signs of major changes are becoming visible in external and internal monetary policy, the implementation of which is the responsibility of the Banco de Portugal (which was nationalised in 1974), as represented by the board, but only within the framework set by policy guidelines determined by the government and the Minister of Finance. In addition to the board of the Banco de Portugal, a number of ministries and credit institutions as well as the autonomous regions of Madeira and the Azores are represented in the council of the central bank.

Mandatory lending ceilings were the most important monetary policy instrument used before March 1990. Since then, indirect methods, such as reformed minimum reserve requirements and the pursuit of an interest rate policy through open market operations, have come to play a more prominent role in controlling the growth of non-banks' liquid assets. Direct controls of the banks' lending rates were abolished in September 1988 (and those on the rates for housing loans in March 1989). Where the banks' deposit rates are concerned, the minimum interest on time deposits with maturities of more than 180 days to one year as well as the maximum interest on sight deposits (in the order of one-third of the interest on time deposits) are still in effect today.

Act No. 337 of 30 October 1990 increased the central bank's autonomy in respect of its monetary policy decisions. In particular, the central bank can no longer be called upon directly to finance the public deficit. Apart from the traditional capability it has to grant limited non-interest bearing cash advances, the central bank is permitted to purchase marketable treasury bills from the government solely at agreed market terms and conditions.

Since the beginning of 1991, the banks have been required to hold minimum reserves in the order of 17% of their financial liabilities at the central bank. Part of these reserves bear interest at the current rate. The actual minimum reserves must be maintained at the specified level on average for a period of about one week, and overlap the reference period for the required reserves on three business days. For purposes of bringing influence to bear on bank liquidity and the money market rates, the central bank either withdraws liquidity by issuing money market paper or provides liquidity in the form of reverse repurchase agreements at the beginning of each reserve period.

April 1992 saw the participation of the central bank in the exchange rate mechanism of the EMS within a wider margin of fluctuation (±6%), which was widened to ±15% on 3 August 1993.

Under the provisions of Act No. 51/84 of 11 February 1984, Banco de Portugal – together with the Minister of Finance – is also responsible for the supervision of all credit institutions.

Structure of the banking system and the market shares of the individual categories of banks

The number of more or less universal-type banks rose from 16 to 29 between the end of 1983 and the end of 1989. 24 of these institutions, which accounted for about 58% of the balance sheet total of all credit institutions, were depository institutions, while three were major savings banks with a combined share of about 29% and two were investment banks with a combined share of some 4%; together, these institutions accounted for more than 90% of the balance sheet total of all credit institutions. The 12 small local savings banks were of virtually no significance, with a share of less than 1% in the balance sheet total of all credit institutions. After the revocation of restrictive provisions in 1982, the number of agricultural credit co-operatives, by contrast, rose from 138 to 222 in 1988, while their share in the total deposits of all credit institutions climbed from 1% to more than 3% in the same period.

The remainder is accounted for by a great number of smaller specialised credit institutions, which rose from 22 in March 1987 to 207 at the end of 1989. These institutions are for the most part investment, leasing and factoring companies, and many were established by domestic and foreign banks.

Depository institutions

Nine of the 24 (at the time of writing) depository institutions were nationalised banks that belonged to the public sector. They held some 50% of the deposits of all credit institutions, although this proportion was beginning to decline. Their share in lending business was slightly smaller, because the private depository institutions (both domestic and foreign), including banks engaged predominantly in investment banking, had been extremely active in this field and had benefited, until spring 1990, from transitional regulations on their lending ceilings which had given them a slight advantage over the nationalised banks.

Seven of the nine nationalised banks were scheduled to be privatised in full in subsequent years. So far, only minority holdings have been sold. Two institutions with weak capital structures have meanwhile become subsidiaries of Caixa Geral de Depositos, the leading state savings and investment bank, and the public investment bank, Banco de Fomento e Exterior, respectively, which now form the cores of two large public banking groups.

The leading, formerly nationalised depository institution, which takes second place only to Caixa Geral de Depositos, was the Banco Portugués do Atlantico. The others, listed in descending order as at the end of 1989, were Banco Espirito Santo e Comercial de Lisboa, Banco Pinto e Sottomayor, Banco Nacional Ultramarino (in which Caixa Geral de Depositos acquired a majority holding of 60% in 1988), Banco Borges e Irmao (which, together with the credit guarantee company Cosec, became part of a group under the lead of the public investment bank Banco de Formento e Exterior in 1989), Uniao dos Bancos Portugueses (which has been partly privatised), Banco Totta e Acores (likewise partly privatised), Banco Fonsecas e Burnay and Banco Comercial dos Acores.

Except for Banco Comercial dos Acores, each of these nationalised and now partly reprivatised institutions maintains a network of between 100 and 140 branch offices which are distributed throughout Portugal. They all have a broad range of banking services on offer for both corporate and individual clients. Their strength is based on their ability to obtain funding at low cost through the savings, sight and time deposits they carry. The rate of return on their capital nevertheless leaves much to be desired, because a legacy from the past, namely the inadequate yield on some assets, has caused their interest margin to be lower than that of most of the newly established private depository institutions. In addition, they have a higher ratio of operating costs to the business volume. The government regards the step-by-step privatisation of these nationalised institutions as a way of improving their efficiency and strengthening their capital base through easier access to the capital market.

The sector comprising the private depository institutions, which had expanded to include 15 institutions by the end of 1989, has been developing very dynamically. Three of the five private depository institutions operating with Portuguese capital were established as late as 1986, but recorded high rates of growth in both lending and deposit business, namely Banco Comercial Portugués (BCP), Banco Internacional de Credito and Banco de Comercio e Industria (which has been under the control of Banco Santander in Spain and Royal Bank of Scotland since 1989). The most successful of these institutions is BCP, which had a network of 61 branch offices at the end of 1989 and which intends to establish a further 60 small offices in the vicinity of businesses and in residential areas. The other two leading private depository institutions, which initially concentrated on investment banking, are likewise well on the way towards developing a nationwide network of at least 100 branch offices.

Institutional links between the domestic banking system and countries abroad

Almost all formerly nationalised banks have foreign branches or representative offices in both the United States and the United Kingdom. Other regions in which they are well represented are France, where Banco Pinto e Sottomayor and Banco Portugués do Atlantico, in particular (which both conduct business primarily with Portuguese emigrants), are represented, as well as Hong Kong, Macao and southern Africa.

Seven of the ten foreign depository institutions established in the form of Portuguese subsidiaries or branches of banks from abroad were licensed only in 1984. The remaining three are institutions which were not nationalised in 1975, namely Crédit Franco Portugais, Lloyds Bank and Banco do Brasil. The first two enjoy a special status because they have long been represented in Portugal and because they – unlike the other foreign depository institutions – have extensive branch office networks there.

Investment banks

This category comprising two rather narrowly defined investment banks must be distinguished from that of the depository institutions, even though the legal distinctions have become minimal. Although they may accept sight and time deposits in the same way as the depository institutions, and although they have also been entitled since 1983 to grant short term loans, they conduct solely medium and long term lending business in practice. Only one-third of their funding is derived from deposit business, while two-thirds are accounted for by share capital, bond issues, borrowing abroad and interbank funds.

The leading bank in this category is the government-owned Banco de Fomento e Exterior mentioned earlier. In addition to granting medium and long term loans, it is responsible for the issue of securities, for the acquisition of participating interests, for project advice and, finally, for the financing of both external trade and economic co-operation with developing countries, not least with former Portuguese colonies in Africa. The second institution in this category is the very much smaller, but dynamically growing private Banco Portugués de Investimento, which was established as an investment bank in 1985. It is particularly active in the field of investment banking, and is in involved in privatisation. It has four foreign financial institutions among its private shareholders.

Major savings banks

A category of considerable significance is that comprising three major savings banks (which have a market share of some 29%). The lion's share is accounted for by Caixa Geral de Depositos, which carries one-quarter of all deposits held by Portuguese credit institutions, and is by far the largest bank or banking group in Portugal.

At the end of 1989, this institution, which was established in 1876, had more than 360 branch offices and also accepted deposits via the country's more than 800 post offices. Under its by-laws, which were approved by legislative act on 5 April 1969, the security of all its deposits is guaranteed by the government. Primarily, Caixa Geral de Depositos grants medium and long term loans for residential construction, to producing enterprises and to electricity generating companies, and it keeps a large portfolio of government securities. It has a strong position in deposit business, and thus plays a leading role in interbank transactions. As has already been mentioned, Caixa Geral de Depositos also has majority holdings in Banco Nacional Ultramarino, in the insurance company Cosec and in two leasing companies as well as in several investment funds and a venture capital company.

The two other major savings banks, Crédito Predial Portugués and Montepio Geral, are of far lesser significance. Whereas the former was one of the institutions nationalised in 1975 and is to be returned to private ownership, Montepio Geral is owned by public welfare institutions. Although the core lending business of these savings banks is still marked by loans for residential construction, they are both attempting – through the use of significant branch office networks and, in part, through the acquisition of participating interests – to diversify their banking business, to the extent that this is permissible under the provisions of the Savings Bank Act.

Agricultural credit co-operatives

The sector formed by the *caixas de crédito agricola* (agricultural credit co-operatives) is of minor importance, but it has been growing since the abolition in 1982 of a number of restrictive provisions brought a turn for the better. 1984 saw the creation of a central institution, Caixas Central de Crédito Agricola, for the 222 (in 1988) credit co-operatives. It manages the liquidity surpluses of the individual credit co-operatives and opens up additional funding opportunities for the sector as a whole.

Specialised credit institutions

The category of specialised credit institutions includes a great number of various types of institutions established in the legal form of *sociedadas financeira Portuguesa* (Portuguese financial institutions), which are subject to special legal requirements and to general supervision by Banco de Portugal. Irrespective of the fact that the number of institutions has been rising rapidly, this category's relative importance in terms of both the three major categories of universal banks – to which, incidentally, there are manifold capital links – and that of the agricultural credit co-operatives has remained small, however. These institutions were promoted by an exemption from the minimum reserve requirements (which has since been partially revoked) and by the abolition of lending ceilings in spring 1990.

The number of investment companies had increased to 20 by the end of 1989. With the sole exception of

Sociedada Financeira Portuguesa, which was established at the beginning of the 1970s and which had subsequently been nationalised, they were all institutions established only recently by private shareholders or by domestic and foreign credit institutions. In principle, investment companies are not permitted to accept deposits, so that they obtain their funding largely through bonds, interbank credit and borrowing abroad. They acquire participating interests in industrial enterprises, grant medium and long term loans, conduct all types of securities transactions and also provide financial consultancy services.

Some of the institutions under foreign ownership were probably established solely because new licences for private banks were issued only very restrictively in the last few years. It is therefore to be expected in the medium term that a number of these investment companies will be converted into universal banks in the course of the creation of the single European financial market.

The last few years have also seen a rapid growth of leasing business, a sector which numbered 17 companies towards the end of 1989. Most of the leasing companies are subsidiaries of banks, which are not permitted to conclude such contracts direct, or of investment companies. Leasing transactions now account for more than 3% of the balance sheet total of all credit institutions.

At the end of 1989, there was one institution specialising in the financing of regional development, six factoring companies, 20 venture capital companies and 61 companies specialising in the management of investment funds, pension funds and other securities portfolios (14 of which were insurance companies) as well as a further 82 financial institutions with a variety of specialities.

Insurance companies are not counted amongst specialised credit institutions. Private ownership has again been possible since 1984. There are now more than 50 insurance companies, half of which are foreign. However, almost three-quarters of all business is still conducted by the eight nationalised insurance companies. The interests of the insurance sector are represented by the Instituto de Seguros de Portugal. Government supervision of the insurance sector is vested in a special division of the Ministry of Finance.

Associations of the banking sector and their members

The only banking association of any major significance is the Associacão Portuguesa de Bancos, the membership of which comprises the major depository institutions and investment banks. It represents the banking sector *vis-à-vis* the government, and is itself a member of the Fédération Bancaire de la Communauté Européenne in Brussels. The agricultural credit cooperatives are members of the Federaçao Nacional das Caixas de Crédito Agricola Mutuo CRL (FENACEM), which was established in 1978.

12 Greece

General outline

As in the case of Spain and Portugal, the main driving force behind a number of essential adjustment processes in Greece is the agreed integration of the banking system into the European financial market by the end of 1992, and by 1995 at the latest. However, it was not until 1987/88 that these adjustment processes set in, even though Greece became a member of the European Community as long ago as 1 January 1981. The tendencies towards a renewal have also been strictly limited by the need for a monetary financing, in an inflationary environment, of a public deficit that has been exceptionally high for years and that has risen even further recently. In addition, the fact must be taken into consideration that, until very recently, the Greek banking market was constricted by a complicated system of credit and audit regulations, which severely limited both the banks' own initiatives and competition between them. All-encompassing government interventionism has hardly been cut back. An estimated 95% of all domestic banks are subject to direct, or indirect, government control.

For all that, the government controls on lending rates have been abolished, and – with the exception of the basic savings rate, the minimum level of which is still set by the relevant monetary authority, the Bank of Greece – deposit rates, too, are freely negotiable. However, the interest rate mechanism continues to play only a minor role in controlling the expansion of lending and the money stock. Of key significance in this respect are the mandatory minimum reserves, which must be held in the form of not only government securities and loans at special terms and conditions to privileged borrowers but also interest-bearing minimum reserves at the central bank. The minimum reserve requirements do not, therefore, reflect an independent monetary policy, but serve primarily to ensure that the public deficit is financed smoothly and that both small industry and public enterprises have access to subsidised funding.

With the advent of the commencement of the second stage of the economic and monetary union in line with the provisions of the Maastricht Treaty on 1 January 1994, which prohibit any direct lending to the government, the Bank of Greece was confronted with a new challenge with respect to its relations with the government. Another key milestone was passed on 16 May 1994 when all remaining restrictions on capital transactions with other EU member states were lifted at a stroke, so that the floating currency had to be defended through high interest rates.

Greece has not as yet become a member of the exchange rate mechanism of the EMS.

Structure and functions of the Bank of Greece

The Bank of Greece fulfils its functions as the monetary authority within the framework of the government's economic policy strategy. The governor and his two deputies are appointed by the government for four years of office, while the other members of the Central Bank Council are appointed by the public limited company's General

Assembly. Its majority shareholders are public entities.

As the central bank, the Bank of Greece has the sole statutory right to issue banknotes. In addition, it manages the country's monetary reserves, grants loans to both the government and commercial banks, and is responsible for banking supervision.

Apart from the foreign institutions, most banks are controlled, if not owned directly by the government. In cases where the majority of the shares of a bank is held by public entities, by insurance companies, non-profit organisations, etc, government bodies represent the interests of that majority at the respective bank's shareholders' meeting, as has been stipulated in an Act dating back to the 1940s.

Market shares of the individual categories of banks

All in all, the Greek banking sector comprised 40 credit institutions at the end of 1988: 12 Greek commercial banks (of which only three were privately owned) with a share of 58% in the sector's balance sheet total; 19 foreign commercial banks with a share of 11%; and 8 specialised credit institutions with a share of 31%. At the end of 1988, the consolidated balance sheet total came to about Dr 10 755 billion. Given a year-on-year rate of inflation of some 15% at the end of 1989, that total climbed to just under Dr 13 000 by the end of that year. The number employed in the Greek banking sector totalled almost 47 000 at the end of 1988.

Leading commercial banks

An outstanding position within the group of domestic commercial banks is held by the National Bank of Greece, which has a share of about one-third of the market. This is paralleled in the bank's branch network, which accounted for 483 of the total of 1388 commercial bank outlets at the end of 1988. An above-average proportion of these branches is concentrated in the three conurbations of Athens, Piraeus and Thessaloniki. Although the banking system comprised a total of 2789 banking offices at the end of 1988, 906 were outlets of the Postal Savings Bank and 420 were branch offices of the Agricultural Bank, which are not fully comparable with the branch offices of the country's leading universal bank, even though they are included in the total.

Moreover, the corporate group headed by the National Bank of Greece, which was established as early as 1841 and which even had the right to issue banknotes up to 1928, also encompasses the Traders' Credit Bank, the National Investment Bank for Industrial Development SA (ETEVA) and the National Housing Bank SA (EST) – two specialised credit institutions – and a number of other financial institutions, including insurance companies and subsidiary banks abroad. The corporate group thus has a complete range of both traditional and innovative financial services on offer, even though not necessarily directly available through the parent bank itself.

A strong position is also held by the second-largest commercial bank in Greece, the Commercial Bank of Greece, which has a market share of 8.9% and 288 branch offices at the end of 1988. These figures rise to 14.1% and 485 respectively, if the commercial banks controlled by the Commercial Bank of Greece, namely the Ionian Bank of Greece SA (ranking third with 170 branches), the Bank of Attica SA and the Bank of Piraeus SA, as well as the Investment Bank SA, are included. In addition, the corporate group also encompasses a number of other financial institutions, including domestic insurance companies and banking subsidiaries abroad.

The other six commercial banks in Greece, which do not belong to one of the two corporate groups mentioned above, have a combined market share of 10.2% and are of minor significance. Worth mentioning is the Credit Bank, which has a market share of as much as 4.5% and in which Manufacturers Hanover Trust Bank has a minority stake. The Credit Bank dates back to the year 1879 (J F Kostopoulo, Athens).

Specialised credit institutions

There are eight specialised credit institutions which, together, accounted for just under 31% of the balance sheet total of all credit institutions at the end of 1988. What is remarkable is that their share in the deposits carried came to only 27.5%, while that in lending business was almost as high as that of the universal commercial banks, at 49%. This was the result of intentional credit management on the part of the Bank of Greece and the government.

A leading and dynamic role is played by the Agricultural Bank with its 420 branch offices, which accounts for 9.8% of the balance sheet total and for 18.6% of the lending business of all credit institutions. The Agricultural Bank is a body of key significance to the government's agricultural policy, and is therefore subordinate to the Minister of Agriculture.

Another reason for the Agricultural Bank's increasing prominence on the market is its co-operation with what are known as 'credit co-operatives', namely the trading co-operatives responsible mainly for buying and selling agricultural products and for the provision of agricultural machinery and equipment. In lending, these so-called credit co-operatives merely act as intermediaries for the Agricultural Bank (and cannot, therefore, be compared with the credit co-operatives in Germany). Moreover, the Agricultural Bank now has 79 branch offices in the large conurbations, and has thus become a major competitor of the commercial banks in business with clients outside agriculture as such.

The investment banks grant long term loans to large industrial companies as well as to small and medium-sized enterprises, shipping and tourism within the scope of regional development plans which are aimed primarily at the establishment of enterprise zones and the promotion of small and medium-sized business. Their share in total lending came to 6.5%. They raise most of their funding through bond issues. There are three investment banks, in all.

One of these, the Hellenic Bank for Industrial Development SA (ETVA), is under the direct control of the government. The other two are subsidiaries of commercial banks, namely the National Investment Bank for Industrial Development SA (ETEVA), which belongs to the group headed by the National Bank of Greece, and the Investment Bank SA, which is controlled by Commercial Bank of Greece, the country's second-largest commercial bank.

Two institutions, the National Mortgage Bank of Greece (EKTE), which has a nationwide network of branches, and the National Housing Bank SA (EST), play a key role in granting medium and long term loans for residential construction and in financing industrial buildings and hotels. EKTE has a share of some 9% in total lending by all credit institutions. Both mortgage banks refinance themselves through securities issues and through deposits, not least through foreign currency deposits of Greek nationals abroad.

The likewise government-owned Postal Savings Bank with its 906 branch offices is a major institution accepting savings deposits, given that it accounts for 7.4% of all the deposits carried by credit institutions. It is also extremely active in lending business. It not only invests its funds in government securities and at the central bank, but also grants longer term loans to public enterprises and finances housing construction projects of public sector employees. And finally, the Cash Deposit and Loan Office accepts funds required in pending court actions or from public bodies, most of which are reinvested in the public sector.

Presence of foreign banks in Greece

At a combined share of just under 11% of the balance sheet total of all credit institutions in Greece, the 19 foreign banks have gained a quite significant position in the market. Two of these institutions are subsidiaries of foreign banks, while the others are represented by branch offices. Almost all of their total of 50 outlets are in the three major conurbations. The leading position within this category is held by Citibank, which has 14 outlets and a market share of 3%. It plays a key role in financing Greek shipping companies. Other institutions worth mentioning are Bank of America, American Express Bank and Chase Manhattan Bank. Twelve foreign banks come from other EU member countries.

Insurance companies, investment funds and credit card companies are not counted among the credit institutions. The capital of the latter two categories is nevertheless controlled almost completely by banks. In the insurance sector, six companies, which have a combined share of some 50% in total insurance business, are subsidiaries of banks.

Greek banking association

All banks which have their head offices in Greece, as well as all foreign banks that have at least one branch office there, are entitled to become members of the Hellenic Banks' Association in Athens; this is largely the case. The

Greek banking association has been a member of the Fédération Bancaire de la Communauté Européenne in Brussels since 1 January 1981. The credit co-operatives are members of the Hellenic Association of Credit Co-operatives, which has its headquarters in Lannia.

Appendix 1:
The 60 largest European banks (at the end of 1989)

Ranking	Bank	Country	Assets (US$ million)	Capital (US$ million)
1	Crédit Agricole	France	242 075	11 806
2	Banque Nationale de Paris	France	231 543	6 179
3	Crédit Lyonnais	France	210 799	6 699
4	Barclays	United Kingdom	205 799	10 039
5	Deutsche Bank[2,3]	Germany	203 028	8 506
6	National Westminster Bank	United Kingdom	187 371	9 592
7	Société Générale	France	164 798	4 776
8	Centre National des Caisses d'Epargne et de Prévoyance	France	150 709	7 864
9	Dresdner Bank	Germany	145 969	5 425
10	Compagnie Financière de Paribas	France	138 716	6 970
11	Union Bank of Switzerland[2,3]	Switzerland	114 142	7 963
12	Commerzbank	Germany	112 466	3 886
13	Deutsche Genossenschaftsbank	Germany	109 581	2 661
14	Istituto Bancario San Paolo di Torino	Italy	107 664	n/a
15	Swiss Bank Corp[2,3]	Switzerland	105 356	6 168
16	Westdeutsche Landesbank	Germany	104 671	2 775
17	Bayerische Vereinsbank	Germany	102 563	2 474
18	Banca Nazionale del Lavoro[3]	Italy	101 212	3 917
19	Midland Bank	United Kingdom	100 756	4 330
20	Amsterdam-Rotterdam Bank	Netherlands	93 114	3 472
21	Lloyds Bank	United Kingdom	92 795	3 814
22	Bayerische Landesbank[2]	Germany	91 198	1 955
23	Algemene Bank Nederland	Netherlands	90 595	3 392
24	Rabobank Nederland	Netherlands	90 201	5 347
25	Hypo Bank	Germany	90 089	2 433
26	Banca Commerciale Italiana	Italy	88 809	3 419
27	Credit Suisse	Switzerland	88 401	4 910
28	NMB Postbank Group	Netherlands	84 366	2 586
29	Credito Italiano	Italy	75 416	2 497
30	Compagnie Financière de CIC	France	74 751	2 256

31	Banco Bilbao Vizcaya	Spain	70 354	n/a
32	Generale Bank	Belgium	67 947	2 081
33	Norddeutsche Landesbank	Germany	67 770	1 512
34	Banco di Napoli[2,3]	Italy	67 166	n/a
35	Monte dei Paschi di Siena[4]	Italy	n/a	3 626
36	Cassa di Risparmio delle Province Lombarde	Italy	66 564	4 088
37	Kreditanstalt für Wiederaufbau	Germany	65 942	1 902
38	Skandinaviska Enskilda Banken	Sweden	59 048	3 729
39	Groupe des Banques Populaires[4]	France	56 132	n/a
40	Banque Indosuez	France	55 335	1 839
41	Banco di Roma[4]	Italy	n/a	1 308
42	Banque Bruxelles Lambert[5]	Belgium	50 440	1 157
43	PKBanken	Sweden	50 399	2 525
44	SwedBank	Sweden	45 927	1 279
45	Crédit Commercial de France	France	45 619	1 513
46	Südwestdeutsche Landesbank[1,2]	Germany	45 051	n/a
47	Crédit Communal de Belgique	Belgium	44 684	1 103
48	Royal Bank of Scotland Group[5]	United Kingdom	44 514	2 289
49	Svenska Handelsbanken	Sweden	44 467	2 651
50	Creditanstalt-Bankverein[2]	Austria	44 353	1 724
51	ASLK-CGER Bank[2]	Belgium	42 401	940
52	Hessische Landesbank	Germany	41 698	1 037
53	Banco de Santander	Spain	41 483	2 315
54	Banque Française du Commerce Extérieur[2,3]	France	41 037	212
55	Banco Central[4]	Spain	n/a	3 208
56	TSB Group[5]	United Kingdom	40 260	2 928
57	Standard Chartered	United Kingdom	39 781	1 555
58	Kredietbank NV[1]	Belgium	38 849	1 108
59	Banco Español de Crédito	Spain	38 680	2 668
60	Compagnie Bancaire	France	38 143	2 619

Source: Institutional Investor, *June 1990.*

1 31 March 1989.

2 Figures do not include all subsidiaries with participating interests of 50% or more.

3 Not all acquisitions are included.

4 Figures for 31 December 1988.

5 Figures for 30 September (or 31 October) 1989.

Appendix 2: Institutions responsible for banking supervision

Country	*Most important banking supervision bodies*	*Institutional coverage*	
		Deposit-taking institutions	*Other financial institutions*
Belgium	*Commission Bancaire*	*All private law banks and savings banks*	*Collective investment institutions*
Denmark	*Ministry of Industry Financial Services*	*All*	*Investment associations*
France	*Commission Bancaire*	*All*	*Finance companies and specialised financial institutions*
Germany	*Bundesaufsichtsamt für das Kreditwesen Deutsche Bundesbank*	*All*	*All, excluding leasing and factoring companies*
Greece	*Bank of Greece*	*All*	*Specialised credit institutions*
Ireland	*Central Bank of Ireland*	*All licensed banks*	
Italy	*Banca d'Italia*	*All*	*Specialised credit institutions; collective investment institutions*
Luxembourg	*Institut Monétaire Luxembourgeois*	*All*	*Non-bank credit institutions; collective investment institutions*
Netherlands	*De Nederlandsche Bank N V*	*All*	*Mortgage banks and two specialised capital market institutions*
Portugal	*Banco de Portugal*	*All*	*Other credit institutions and all near-banking institutions*
Spain	*Banco de España Ministry of Finance*	*All, excluding the public banks*	*Collective investment institutions; finance companies; mortgage companies; money market houses and funds leasing*
United Kingdom	*Bank of England*	*All 'authorised deposit-taking institutions'*	

Source: Pecchioli, Rinaldo M, Bankenaufsicht in den OECD-Ländern: Entwicklungen und Probleme, *Baden-Baden, 1989, a translation of 'Prudential supervision in banking', OECD, 1987.*

Appendix 3:
List of European banking and other financial associations

Members of the Comité des Organisations Professionelles du Crédit de la Communauté Européenne (COC)

1. Fédération Bancaire de la Communauté Européenne
   Rue Montoyer 10 – 1040 Bruxelles
   Tel: 508 37 11 Fax: 502 79 66

2. Groupement Européen des Caisses d'Epargne
   Avenue de la Renaissance 12 – 1040 Bruxelles
   Tel: 739 16 11 Fax: 736 09 55

3. Groupement Européen des Banques Coopératives
   Rue de la Science 23–25 – 1040 Bruxelles
   Tel: 230 11 24 Fax: 230 06 49

4. Confédération Internationale du Crédit Populaire (CICP)
   Rue de l'Industrie 40 – 1040 Bruxelles
   Tel: 513 14 59 / 513 39 52
   Fax: 511 03 46
   Rue Leblanc 5 – 75511 Paris Cedex 15
   Tel: 331 40 39 60 00
   Fax: 331 40 39 60 01

5. Fédération Hypothécaire auprès de la Communauté Européenne
   Av. de la Joyeuse Entrée 14-Bte2 – 1030 Bruxelles
   Tel: 230 25 51 Fax: 230 64 11

6. European Federation of Building Societies
   Dottendorfer Strasse 32 – 53129 Bonn
   Tel: +49 228 23 90 41
   Fax: +49 228 23 90 46

7. EUROFINAS (European Federation of Finance Houses Associations)
   Avenue de Tervueren 267-Bte10 – 1150 Bruxelles
   Tel: 771 21 08 Fax: 770 75 96

8. Fédération des Bourses Européenne
   Rue du midi 2, 5ème – 1000 Bruxelles
   Tel: 513 05 18/511 83 35
   Fax: 512 49 05/514 55 81

9. European Group of Financial Institutions
   European Economic Interest Grouping
   Rue Defacqz 125 – 1050 Bruxelles
   Tel: 534 58 13 Fax: 534 50 44

10. European Federation of Retirement Provision
    Rue de Pierres 29 – 1000 Bruxelles
    Tel: 502 54 66 Fax: 502 74 77

11. Fédération Européenne des Fonds & Sociétés d'Investissement
    Square de Meeùs 20 – 1040 Bruxelles
    Tel: 513 39 69 Fax: 513 26 43

12. Comité Européen des Assurances (CEA)
    3 bis rue de la Chaussée d'Antin – 75009 Paris
    Tel: 331 48 24 66 00
    Fax: 331 47 70 03 75

Observers:
- Eurocheque International, 1050 Bruxelles
- Eurocard International SA, 1050 Bruxelles
- Visa International Service Association, London
- European Council for Payment Systems (ECPS), Bruxelles
- SWIFT, 1310 La Hulpe

Bibliography

Annual accounts and annual reports, as well as monthly or quarterly reports, of various central banks, credit institutions and banking supervisory authorities in the EU countries

Banca d'Italia:
Italian Credit Structures – Efficiency, competition and controls, London, 1984
Proceedings of the Workshop on Payment System Issues in the Perspectives of European Monetary Unification, workshop in Perugia on 22/23 November 1990, Rome, November 1991

Banco Bilbao Vizcaya:
Situacion 1989 – The Spanish Economy in 1988 and 1989, Bilbao, January 1990

Bank for International Settlements:
Annual Reports, Basle
Quarterly and half-yearly press releases on international banking and financial market developments, Basle
Recent Innovations in International Banking, Basle, April 1986
The Orientation of Monetary Policy and the Monetary Policy Decision-Making Process, Basle, April 1981

Banque de France:
La Monnaie en 1989, Paris, 1990

Beutler, B, Bieber, R, Pipkorn, J and Streil, J:
Das Recht der Europäischen Gemeinschaften – Textsammlung, Baden-Baden, serial publication

Bibliography

Bingham, T R G:

'Banking and monetary policy', *Trends in Banking Structure and Regulation in OECD Countries* (series), OECD, Paris, 1985

Bröder, E-G:

'Are banks ready for 1992?', *The International Economy,* March/April 1989

Bröker, G:

'Competition in banking in OECD countries', *Trends in Banking Structure and Regulation in OECD Countries* (series), OECD, Paris, 1989

Brown and Bowman (eds):

The International Banking Centres, London, 1982

Büschgen, H E and Schneider, U H (eds):

'Der europäische Binnenmarkt 1992 – Auswirkungen auf die deutsche Finanzwirtschaft' (The single European market in 1992 – its impact on the German financial sector), *Wertpapiermitteilungen*, Frankfurt am Main, 1990

Committee on Banking Regulations and Supervisory Practices ('Basle Supervisors' Committee'):

'Report on international developments in banking supervision', Report 1 ff, Basle, 1983 ff

Dale, R:

'The EEC approach to capital adequacy for investment firms', *The Journal of International Securities Markets,* vol 4, Autumn 1990

Deutsche Bundesbank:

Verzeichnis der Kreditinstitute, Frankfurt am Main, 1990 and 1992

Dräger, C and Späth, L (eds):

'Internationales Währungssystem und weltwirtschaftliche Entwicklung – eine Herausforderung an die internationale Wirtschaftskooperation' (The international monetary system and global economic development – a challenge to international economic cooperation), *Dokumentation des Malenter Symposiums VII*, vol 12, Dräger Foundation, Baden-Baden, 1988

Duwendag, D (ed):

'Europa-Banking – Bankpolitik im Europäischen Finanzraum

und währungspolitische Integration' (Banking in Europe – banking policy in the European financial area and monetary policy integration), *Schriften zur monetären Ökonomie*, vol 27, Baden-Baden, 1988

European Communities, Commission/Council:

Conference of Financial Conglomerates, Brussels/Luxembourg, 1988

Kreditinstitute – Zusammenstellung der EG-Rechtsakte und Vorschläge, Brussels/Luxembourg, 1989

'Liste der Kreditinstitute gemäß Art. 3 Abs. 7 und Art. 10 Abs. 22 der Richtlinie 77/780/EWG' (List of credit institutions covered by the provisions of paragraph 7 of Article 3 and paragraph 22 of Article 10 of Directive 77/780/EEC – as at 31 December 1988), 10th edition, *Amtsblatt der Europäischen Gemeinschaften*, 90/C107, Brussels/Luxembourg, 30 April 1990 (and later editions)

Vertrag über die Europäische Union, Brussels/Luxembourg, 1992

Europäische Sparkassenvereinigung:

Bank- und Finanzrecht der EG, Brussels, autumn 1991

Fair, D and de Boissieu, C (eds):

Financial Institutions in Europe under New Competitive Conditions, Colloqium in Nice on 12–14 October 1989, Société Universitaire Européenne de Recherches Financières (SUERF), Dordrecht/Boston/Lancaster, 1990

Faßbender, H and Leichtfuß, R:

'Banking im neuen Europa: Zwischenbilanz (I und II)' (Banking in the new Europe – intermediate assessment (I and II)), *Die Bank*, nos 5 and 6, 1990

Franke, G and von Schimmelmann, W (eds):

Banken im Vorfeld des Europäischen Binnenmarktes, Wiesbaden, 1989

Gil, G:

'Spanish financial system', *Economic Studies No. 29*, 3rd edition, Bank of Spain, Madrid, 1984

Gilbody, J:

The UK Monetary Financial System, London/New York, 1988

Harrington, R:

'Asset and liability management by banks', *Trends in Banking*

Structure and Regulation in OECD Countries (series), OECD, Paris, 1987

Hendrie, A:

'Banking in the EEC, 1988: Structures and sources of finance', *Financial Times Business Information*, 6th edition, London, 1988

Kaufmann, G G (ed):

Banking Structures in Major Countries, Boston/Dordrecht/London, 1992

Klein, D K R:

'Bankenstruktur und Geldpolitik' (Banking structures and monetary policy), *Zeitschrift für das gesamte Kreditwesen*, no 1, Frankfurt am Main, 1 January 1986

'Erkennen, wohin der Zug im Kreditgewerbe abfährt' (Recognising the direction developments in the banking sector are taking), *Handelsblatt*, Sonderbeilage Banken International (special supplement on international banks), 25 April 1985

'Europas Universalbanken sind leistungsfähiger als manche hochspezialisierte Kreditinstitute' (Europe's universal banks are more efficient than many of the highly specialised credit institutions), *Handelsblatt*, Sonderbeilage Euromärkte (special supplement on Euro-markets). 27 November 1986

'International banking in the 1980s', *UMBC Economic Review*, vol XIX, no 1. Kuala Lumpur, 1983

'L'Internationalisation des activités bancaires dans les années 1980' (The internationalisation of banking activities in the 1980s), *Eurépargne*, no 11, Luxembourg, 1984

'More competition through less protectionism in banking and related financial services', Fels, G and Sutija, G (eds): *Protectionism and International Banking*, International Conference in Frankfurt am Main on 29–31 October 1987, IW and PACE, London, 1991

'Strategic planning by international banks to cope with uncertainty', Savona, P and Sutija, G (eds): *Strategic Planning in International Banking*, International Conference in Rome on 11–12 May 1984, PACE and ABI, London, 1985

'Structure bancaire et politique monétaire' (Banking structures and monetary policy), *Eurépargne*, no 10, 1986

Kluge, O:

Die Mindestharmonisierung des Bankenrechts in der EG als Wettbewerbsproblem, thesis submitted at the University of Frankfurt, 1989

Krone, B:

'Das griechische Bankwesen' (The Greek banking system), *Bankinformation – Volksbanken, Raiffeisenbanken*, vol 16, no 5, 15 May 1989

Masera, R S:

'Issues in financial regulation: efficiency, stability, information', Fair and de Boissieu, op. cit.

'Monetary and financial markets in Europe: regulation and market forces', *Review of Economic Conditions in Italy*, Banco di Roma, no 1, 1989

The multifunctional group in Italy compared with the universal bank, manuscript, April 1990

Moody's Investors Service:

Moody's System Study (ongoing studies of national banking systems and the ratings of individual banks), New York

Mura, J (ed):

Kreditinstitute im europäischen Binnenmarkt 1993, Gesellschaft zur Förderung der Wissenschaftlichen Forschung über das Spar- und Girowesen, Stuttgart, 1990

Obst and Hintner:

Geld-, Bank- und Börsenwesen, Kloten, N and von Stein, J H (eds), 38th edition, Stuttgart, 1988

OECD:

Arrangements for the Regulation and Supervision of Securities Markets, report by the Committee on Financial Markets, Paris, 1989

Bank Profitability, Financial Statements of Banks with Methodological Country Notes 1980–1984, Paris, 1987

Bank Profitability – Statistical Supplement, financial statements of banks 1981–85/1982–88 (annual supplements), Paris

Banks under Stress, Expert Meeting on Banking Structure and Regulation on 10–11 September 1990, Paris, 1992

Financial Market Trends, special feature: 'International trade in services and para-banking services', no 40, Paris, May 1988

International Trade in Services: Banking, Identification and Analysis of Obstacles, Paris, 1984

International Trade in Services: Securities, Paris, 1987
Trends in Banking in OECD Countries, Committee on Financial Markets, Expert Group on Banking (general report on monographic publications published as part of *Trends in Banking Structure and Regulation in OECD Countries* (series), Paris), Paris, 1985
OECD financial statistics:
Financial Statistics Monthly, part 1, Paris
Financial Accounts of OECD Countries, part 2, Paris
Non-financial Enterprises Financial Statements, part 3, Paris
Methodological Supplement, Paris, 1990 (and earlier issues)
Peat, Marwick, Mitchell & Co:
Banking in United Kingdom, London, 1987
Banking in Germany, 7th edition, 1986
Banking in France, 1979
Banking in The Netherlands, 1979
Banking in Spain, 1980
Pecchioli, R M:
Bankenaufsicht in den OECD-Ländern: Entwicklungen und Probleme, German (partially revised) translation of the OECD monographic publication: 'Prudential supervision in banking', Baden-Baden, 1989
'Prudential supervision in banking', *Trends in Banking Structure and Regulation in OECD Countries* (series), OECD, Paris, 1987
'The internationalism of banking, the policy issues', *Trends in Banking Structure and Regulation in OECD Countries* (series), OECD, Paris, 1983
Presse- und Informationsamt der Bundesregierung:
'Vertrag über die Europäische Union' (Treaty on European Union), *Bulletin*, no 16, p 113, Bonn, 12 February 1992
Rand McNally & Company:
The Rand McNally Bankers Directory, 1987 (final edition)
Rehm, H (ed):
Perspektiven für den Europäischen Bankenmarkt, Verband öffentlicher Banken, Bonn, 1989
Reimann, W:
Öffentliche Banken in der Zeit, Bonn, 1992
Remsperger, H and Angenendt, U:
'Strukturwandel im deutschen Universalbankensystem' (Struc-

tural changes in the German universal banking system), *Die Bank*, no 10, 1990

Revell, J R S:

'Banking and electronic funds transfers', *Trends in Banking Structure and Regulation in OECD Countries* (series), OECD, Paris, 1983

Salomon Brothers:

European Banking Integration in 1992: The Competitive Challenges Facing U.S. Multinational Banks, June 1989

Multinational Money Center Banking: The Evolution of a Single European Banking Market – Banks Transform the Distribution of Selected Insurance Products, New York, September 1990

Schneider, Hellwig and Kingsman:

The German Banking System, 4th edition, Frankfurt am Main, 1986

Schneider, U H:

'Das Aufsichtsrecht der Allfinanz-Konzerne' (Supervision law applicable to 'one-stop' financial groups), *Wertpapiermitteilungen*, no 40, vol 44, 6 October 1990

The legal possibilities and barriers regarding overlapping activities between the various sectors in the finance industry, particularly the banks and insurance companies, and the formation of conglomerates in the industry, manuscript, Mainz, 1987

Schroeder-Hohenwarth, H C and Remsperger, H:

'Zur Position des deutschen Kreditgewerbes im EG-Binnenmarkt' (The situation of the German banking sector in the single European market), Duwendag (ed): *Europa-Banking*, Baden-Baden, 1988

Stein, J:

Das Bankwesen in Deutschland, 16th edition, Bundesverband deutscher Banken Köln, Cologne, March 1990 (annual publication)

Steinherr, A and Gilibert, P-L:

'Regulating the European financial sector beyond 1992', *The Journal of International Securities Markets*, vol 3, winter 1989 (Part 1), and vol 4, spring 1990 (Part 2)

The City Directory 1989, published in association with the Institute of Directors, London, 1989

The Economist publications:
'France' in series *European Financial Centres*, no 1, London, 1989
'Italy' in series *European Financial Centres*, no 2, London, 1989
'Spain' in series *European Financial Centres*, no 3, London, 1989
Thießen, Friedrich:
'Standorttheorie für internationale Finanzzentren' (Approach to the assessment of the locational advantages and disadvantages of international financial centres), *Untersuchungen zur Wirtschaftspolitik*, vol 74, Institut für Wirtschaftspolitik an der Universität zu Köln, Cologne, 1988
Verband öffentlicher Banken:
'Kreditwirtschaftlich wichtige Vorhaben der EG' (EC projects of significance to banking), *Schriftenreihe des Verbandes öffentlicher Banken*, Bonn, March 1992
'Perspektiven für den Europäischen Bankenmarkt' (Prospects of the European banking market), *Berichte und Analysen*, vol 10, Bonn, 1988

Index